THE REFORM OF
SECONDARY EDUCATION

THE REFORM OF SECONDARY EDUCATION

A Report to the Public and the Profession

THE NATIONAL COMMISSION ON THE
REFORM OF SECONDARY EDUCATION
B. FRANK BROWN, Chairman

ESTABLISHED BY THE CHARLES F. KETTERING FOUNDATION

McGRAW-HILL BOOK COMPANY
New York   St. Louis   San Francisco   Düsseldorf
London   Mexico   Sydney   Toronto

Library of Congress Cataloging in Publication Data

National Commission on the Reform of Secondary
  Education.
  The reform of secondary education.

  1. Education, Secondary—United States.
I. Title.
LA222.N33   1973   373.73   73-18002
ISBN 0-07-046049-3
ISBN 0-07-046050-7 (pbk.)

CONTENTS

NATIONAL COMMISSION ON THE REFORM OF SECONDARY EDUCATION

SAMUEL BASKIN

President, Union for Experimenting Colleges and Universities
Yellow Springs, Ohio

PETER CLIFFORD

Executive Secretary, Secondary School Department, The National Catholic Educational Association
Washington, D. C.

JASON CONVISER

President, Student Council, East Evanston Township High School
Evanston, Illinois

SARAH A. DAVIS

Director, Volunteer and Tutorial Programs, Los Angeles Unified City School District
Los Angeles, California

WILLIAM A. DU PRÉE

Principal, Hughes High School
Cincinnati, Ohio

CLAUDIA SCHEDLEY	President, State of Ohio Vocational Industrial Clubs of America Valley Forge High School Parma, Ohio
JOHN A. STANAVAGE	Executive Secretary, Commission on Secondary Schools, North Central Association of Colleges and Secondary Schools Chicago, Illinois
CAROLYN STEELMAN	Chairman, English Department Crossland High School Camp Springs, Maryland
LOUIS G. ZEYEN	Senior Associate Secretary, American Association of School Administrators; Director, National Academy for School Executives Arlington, Virginia
B. FRANK BROWN	*Chairman*—Director, Information and Services Program, Institute for Development of Educational Activities, Inc., An Affiliate of the Charles F. Kettering Foundation Melbourne, Florida

STAFF OF THE COMMISSION

W. Arthur Darling	Research & Writing Assistant
Phyllis H. Dexter	Secretary to the Commission
Linda J. Field	Report Coordinator
Emmat F. Frauman	Media Specialist
James R. Ryoland	Administrative Assistant
Linda D. Schmitt	Assistant to the Secretary
Melba F. Smith	Office Manager

The High School in Historical Perspective

A Stormy Petrel

A petrel is usually defined as something whose coming portends trouble or strife. When the high school is examined as an institution from its point of origin to where it is, it is seen to be the stormiest of petrels. The existence of the high school has always been controversial and often turbulent. If an institution could speak, the high school would periodically breathe a sigh and say, "One more peril passed."

Beginning with Benjamin Franklin's proposals for the education of youth, the very idea of a high school created a furor. In 1820, there arose an unprecedented social storm on the part of middle-class and labor groups in their clamor for the use of public funds to support high schools. The agitation lasted for decades.

High schools were dragged through an unheard of arena of legal battles in the 1860s over the issue of whether or not school boards had the right to levy taxes for the support of high schools. This volatile issue was not settled until the

Supreme Court of Michigan affirmed this right in the famous
Kalamazoo case (1874).

By 1880, the high school had entered another crisis caused
by an overemphasis on traditional humanism and lack of attention to science, English, and the modern languages. This
crisis intensified in 1888 when Charles W. Eliot, president of
Harvard University, brought the weaknesses of the system to
public attention in an epochal address in Washington, D.C.
The wave of criticism against the schools was climaxed by the
formation of the "Committee of Ten" which subsequently
recommended the first major reforms in the high schools.

It was near the end of the nineteenth century before the
high school began to take its place as a normal continuation
of education beyond the elementary school. While the elementary school maintained a peaceful existence throughout a
century of turmoil, the high school continued to be the center
of controversy even after the social and legal battles over its
survival were resolved.

By 1910, secondary education had become the focus of
another uproar, this time from within the educational profession itself because of accusations that high school students
were either becoming involved in "suicidal specialization" or
taking so many courses that they were acquiring only an
"excessive smattering" of the curriculum. In an effort to cope
with this issue, the National Education Association, in 1912,
appointed the Commission on the Reorganization of Secondary
Education which, after six years of study and deliberations,
defined the objectives of secondary education in a set of Seven
Cardinal Principles. This action rallied the profession around
a united program of studies based on these objectives.

However, by 1930 another tempest was raging over the
issue of whether progressive education was preparation for
college entrance. This quandry culminated in the Eight-Year
Study. In the interim between establishment of the Eight-Year
Study and its report, the Education Policies Commission of

the National Education Association and the American Association of School Administrators found it necessary to issue a second definition of purposes in 1938.

For the next twenty years high schools, for the first time, were relatively free of controversy. They had reached public legitimacy. Then, in 1959, James Bryant Conant published his report, *The American High School Today*, with twenty-one recommendations for change. While the Conant report generated discussion and debate, it was, in the main, noncontroversial. Perhaps its greatest impact was to offer a ready-made plan of action for National Defense Education Act funds, which became available as a result of the launching of Sputnik.

Despite a tempestuous history in which it had moved from crisis to crisis, the high school was ill-prepared for the widespread turbulence which began in 1968 with the White Plains (New York) High School Incident (the first recorded student demonstration (race riot) at the high school level—Tuesday, March 26, 1968)—and the succeeding years of student dissent, unrest, and racial discord. These influences, coupled with countless court decisions, have radically changed the high schools' student bodies, and the attitudes of students on racial, cultural, and socioeconomic matters. Neither the schools' altered clientele nor restricted authority currently matches the traditional mode of operation.

It was against this backdrop that the Charles F. Kettering Foundation decided that it was time for new reforms and subsequently organized and sponsored a national commission to re-examine the goals, programs, and directions of secondary education.

In July 1972, the Foundation, through its affiliate the Institute for Development of Educational Activities, Inc., authorized the establishment of the National Commission on the Reform of Secondary Education. In making the announcement, Robert G. Chollar, president of the Foundation, described the purpose and charged the Commission to:

... make a comprehensive examination of secondary education and provide the American public with a clear, factual
picture of their secondary schools, indicating where and
how they can be altered to better serve the nation's young
people.

The Commission was constituted after consultations with
the professional organizations most involved in the education
of the nation's youth. Individuals selected for membership
were those who could speak for the points of view of the
American Association of School Administrators, National
School Boards Association, Chief State School Officers Association, National Association of Secondary School Principals,
National Congress of Parents and Teachers, the National
Catholic Educational Association, and the North Central Association of Colleges and Secondary Schools. Other areas of
representation included a state legislature, the teaching profession, teacher training institutions, volunteer and tutorial
programs, career education, higher education, high school student bodies, and the private sector.

To augment the work of the Commission, national panels
of teachers, parents, students, and administrators (superintendents and principals) were established. The staff of the
Commission randomly selected 200 persons, with representation from every state, for membership on each of the national
panels. As the work of the Commission progressed, the panels
were surveyed periodically about various aspects of secondary
education. Results of the surveys were compiled and reported
to the full Commission or the appropriate subcommittee.

The work of the Commission was conducted through monthly
hearings in various sections of the continental United States.
Able consultants of varying professions and persuasions were
engaged to participate in the deliberations. Monthly sessions
were combined with on-site visits to schools, interviews, and
discussions with students, teachers, and administrators. The
endeavor of the Commission was further supported by the

efforts of subcommittees consisting of Commission members who contributed enormous amounts of time to the project. Subcommittee work involved additional visits to schools and school systems around the country as well as seminars abroad. This report is a result of these investigations and of many days and weeks of discussion.

While the report contains a number of recommendations that lead toward reform of the high schools, the Commission is keenly aware that solutions to many of the problems of secondary education are elusive and will continue to be so for a long time.

We know that schools can function effectively in a changing society only to the extent that they adjust to its needs and exploit in its service emerging advances in instructional methodology and techniques. The incentive for continuous innovation will come from achievement and success.

The Commission does not expect its recommendations for reform to command unanimous approval. It does hope they will evoke discussion, debate, controversy, and action. Nor does the Commission anticipate or even think it desirable for its recommendations to bring peace and harmony to the nation's secondary schools. An institution which is designed to serve society by educating its adolescents can be expected to, and should, remain controversial. It should continue to live up to its reputation as a stormy petrel.

B. FRANK BROWN, *Chairman*

ACKNOWLEDGMENTS

The members of the Commission acknowledge their indebtedness to the many individuals who met with the Commission to assist in its deliberations and to the various school systems which opened their doors for visits.

A special note of appreciation is due the following:

Robert G. Chollar, president, Charles F. Kettering Foundation, and Samuel G. Sava, executive director, Institute for Development of Educational Activities, Inc., for funding the Commission and allowing it to function as an independent agency.

Sidney P. Marland, former United States Commissioner of Education and present assistant secretary of Health, Education, and Welfare, for his open support of and assistance to the Commission's investigations.

The Citizens' Advisory Council on the Status of Women for their help with that part of the report dealing with stereotyping by sex in secondary curricula.

Executives of the National Broadcasting Company, American Broadcasting Company, Television Information Office of the National Association of Broadcasters, Children's Television Workshop, British Broadcasting Corporation, and Independent Broadcasting Authority of Britain, for their participation and assistance in the report on the impact of television.

The Gottlieb-Duttweiler Institute of Zurich, Switzerland,

for their cooperation in housing a seminar on international education for the section on global education.

The American Association of School Administrators and the National Association of Secondary School Principals for their cooperation throughout the study and for co-sponsoring summer Institutes for educators to introduce this report.

THE REFORM OF
SECONDARY EDUCATION

PART I

THE SETTING FOR REFORM OF SECONDARY EDUCATION

CHAPTER 1

Rationale
for a New Examination of
Secondary Education

Within the past ten years the cost of the high schools to the taxpayers has doubled. The public expects this more expensive secondary educational system to serve students from a more diverse population. With these changes have come criticisms that have sown seeds of doubt and confusion about the school's effectiveness.

The wave of criticism against the high school has reached the point of overkill. If the high school is to survive as an institution, a concerted effort must be made to solve its many problems. The urgency of the subject should command the attention of public policy and community action.

The larger problems of American society are reflected in the high schools. Education is warped by the tension between a rapidly changing society and a slowly changing school. In an effort to discover the best way to accelerate educational change, millions of dollars have been invested in educational

3

research. Unfortunately, this substantial effort has produced few significant findings and even fewer practical recommendations.

What is needed most is information on how to bring about change of sufficient magnitude to promise better education for all the nation's youth. What is known is that programmatic change requires institutional change, and changing an institution takes time.

In a meeting with the Commission, former United States Commissioner of Education Sidney P. Marland, now Assistant Secretary of Health, Education, and Welfare, proposed a cheerless paradox on the relationship of research and educational change: "The more significant the issue, the less likely the research data."

The End of the Boom in Education

On the horizon, complicating all efforts to move the high schools out of older patterns, is the end of the extraordinary postwar expansion. The educational establishment, which has been the nation's fastest growing enterprise, has stopped growing. This trend can already be felt in the serious oversupply of teachers. George H. Brown, head of the Census Bureau, predicts that by 1985 "we won't need any more new high schools" except, of course, for replacements. With families becoming smaller, the elementary schools are already experiencing reduced enrollments. The nation's birth rate is at its lowest point in history and still declining. No single reason for the declining fertility rate exists. Among explanations that have been offered are economic factors, availability of abortion and contraception, the movement of the population from rural to urban areas, and the new independence of women.

The high schools can no longer grow by increasing the proportion of the population retained into secondary education; virtually the entire high school age cadre for 1981 is already in school. Both the engines of school expansion have stopped, and ten years from now—this is one of the few predictions of the future that can be made with absolute confidence—the total population of American high schools will be smaller than it is today.

The implications are serious for the educational establishment, for teacher training institutions, and for teachers' associations. They are en route to becoming the victims of an economy of declining populations. The most obvious consequence of the decline will be a decrease in the number of youthful new teachers employed. Schools will be unable to bring in large numbers of younger people as they did in the fifties and sixties, and the people brought in during that era will be growing older. The big question is: What can the high schools accomplish at a time when they are getting smaller, fewer youngsters are going through them, and the teachers are growing older? For an institution accustomed to the buoyancy of constant growth, the consequences could be tragic.

The statistics are frightening. According to population projections from the Census Bureau, secondary schools will experience a drop of more than two million in student enrollment between 1973 and 1984. A decline of this magnitude unquestionably implies a reduction in appropriations. It is hard to believe that taxpayers are going to pay as much for smaller schools as they did for larger ones. Educational planners must take these factors into account as they formulate schemes for education.

Even steeper declines in the enrollment of the comprehensive high school may result from the reforms this Commission proposes. With the burgeoning of alternative paths to the diploma, as little as 40 percent of the student population may be graduated from conventional comprehensive high schools. Increasing numbers of students can be expected to use bypass mechanisms or to select from a wide variety of alternatives. The extent to which these bypass mechanisms and alternatives will employ the services of those who are now teachers cannot be predicted at this time.

Teacher Supply and Demand

At best, schools will have to reform through the work of the present staffs, without any great infusion of new blood.

In 1955, the nation was confronted with a teacher shortage approaching a million teachers. Gradually, the job slots filled up, until by the mid-sixties there were enough teachers. Since that time, there has been a growing surplus as the largest college classes in history have been graduated onto the market. The excess reported since 1969 by the NEA Research Division is as follows:

ANNUAL SURPLUS OF NEW TEACHERS

1969	56,000
1970	100,000
1971	111,000
1972	118,000
1973	128,000 (projected)

Today, the teacher training institutions are training two teachers for every position. The educational establishment for the first time in history has a golden opportunity to select rigorously those who are to be trained as teachers.

With decreased demand for teachers, the training institutions should reconsider their procedures, even their function. They no longer operate in a seller's market; they must find out what the secondary schools expect from teachers and plan their training programs accordingly. Their role of leadership as specialists in secondary education is at an end. The focus has shifted from the university level to the local scene.

The Decade of Innovation

The period between 1962 and 1972 can be characterized as a decade of experimentation and innovation in the schools.

This was an era during which a major effort was made to create "strategies for change." The most common strategy was modeled on the work of the Department of Agriculture in the 1930s and 1950s, when improvements in farming technology were introduced through "agricultural agents," whose farms were seen to be more productive than those of less enlightened neighbors. Education, too, would have its "change agents."

This approach created grand opportunities for ambitious educators, who became experts in the internal procedures of private foundations and government grantors. The mere fact that a school had been singled out by a private or governmental foundation gave it prestige in its community. A great deal of activity seemed to occur. In the words of the Ford Foundation's evaluation of its own spending for public school improvement: "The 1960s were a decade of innovation for the schools. Spurred by foundations and later by federal and state governments, public school systems embraced a host of new programs and projects in curriculum, staffing, scheduling, technology, and training."[1]

The Ford analysts concluded that the foundation had invested $30 million in school innovations without any lasting or significant results. "Money alone," they wrote, "seemed not to be decisive in innovative improvement." Most innovations were abandoned "after the departure of the charismatic promoter or with reduction of external funding."

The following innovations attracted the most funding from foundations and the U.S. Office of Education during the decade of innovation:

team teaching	independent study
modular scheduling	learning centers
nongraded schools	open plan schools
programmed learning	language laboratories
individualized instruction	behavioral objectives
computer-assisted instruction	differentiated staffing

The list itself bears out the Ford conclusions; the decade of change and innovation in the schools had little or no lasting effect on the content of school programs or the quality of teaching and learning.

High Schools in Crisis

The American high school has become a beleaguered institution. Everyone agrees that the high schools are in difficulty, but there agreement ceases; even before they arrive at proposals, experts find themselves arguing about what is wrong and about the source and size of the trouble. While educators ponder the problem, the high school environment deteriorates further.

Our large city school systems are on the verge of complete collapse. Two decades ago, the cities operated the best school systems in the United States. Today, these schools are at the bottom in academic accomplishment. Data from the National Assessment of Educational Progress reveal that achievement in schools of the inner city has fallen even below that in schools of the rural South, traditionally the nation's inferior schools.

The coercion of compulsory school attendance is no longer working. Attendance reports from urban school systems show that in many of the large city high schools, fewer than half the enrolled students attend regularly. Average daily attendance as a percentage of enrollment runs as low as 45 percent in some urban schools. Among those who do come to school, tardiness and class cutting are common.

Attendance rates have been deteriorating in suburban schools as well. For example, the percentage of average daily attendance in Florida decreased every year from 1966 to 1972. Spot checks in a number of states indicate that the trend is national and is increasing in severity. For schoolmen, the decline in attendance has further implications. State aid to schools, which has been a rising proportion of school funding, is normally based on average daily attendance. In many state legislatures, lobbyists for school systems are now advocating a change in the aid formulas to permit payment on enrollment "membership" rather than on attendance. Some states have already moved toward the use of the membership factor.

Poor attendance is symptomatic of other trouble within the schools. During the last five years, crime has become part of normal experience in many high schools. Surveys indicate that 64 percent of the nation's school systems now employ people to perform specific police functions. A decade ago, fewer than 10 percent employed any type of security personnel. The size of the security effort can be illustrated by the actions of the Chicago school board, which increased its school police force from 2 to 600 between 1966 and 1973.

The widespread increase in assaults on students and teachers has led to a Safe Schools Act now pending in the Congress. Nobody, ten years ago, would have anticipated a demand for federal legislation to make the schools safe places to attend.

Decline in achievement in urban school systems, a nation-wide decrease in school attendance, and an increase in crime in the schools—such diseases must be diagnosed and cured.

Changes in Mission

Among the sources of the problems of the high schools has been society's insistence on sudden and traumatic changes in their mission.

After the launching of Sputnik, national educational policy, including research and development, was directed toward the advancement of achievement in science and mathematics. The high school was targeted as the institution best able to accomplish this objective.

Social legislation of the early sixties, and the national effort to eliminate poverty and racial discrimination, brought a sudden shift in national policy toward better education for the disadvantaged. The schools, which only six years before had feverishly geared for a substantial concentration in mathematics and science courses, were required to make an abrupt shift in a massive effort to improve the education of the disadvantaged, especially education in basic skills.

Social legislation and administrative action also assigned to the schools responsibility for changing racial attitudes and correcting a broad range of social deficiencies. Now, the prominence of social goals has brought forth a clamor for the schools to recast their priorities and to adjust to individually different outcomes of education.

The American comprehensive high school today must be viewed as an establishment striving to meet the complex demands of a society in the throes of social change, at a time when the school system has become too large as an institution and is literally overrun with a mix of young people from inconsistent social backgrounds. This is a difficult circumstance. The pressure of these forces exhausts the strength of the high school as an organized institution. It must be remembered that the school is only one of the agencies of society and works at the socialization process while striving to accomplish its prime function: the education of youth in both the cognitive and affective domains.

The Deschooling Movement

The effort to "deschool" society started with Paul Goodman's book *Growing Up Absurd: Problems of Youth in Organized Society* (1956).[2] While it is now obvious that Goodman and Edgar Z. Friedenberg were prophetic in their criticisms of the effectiveness of the comprehensive high school, the Commission sees no virtue in the efforts of their disciples to eliminate schools. "Deschooling" may be a useful exercise in scholarly discourse, but it cannot be taken seriously.

The issue is not whether high schools are useful, but what

role they should assume. The Commission recognizes that the primary environment of the child is the home, and that the schools cannot make up for all the deficiencies of the home. This does not mean they can do nothing.

Goals of Secondary Education

Elsewhere in this report, mention is made of the fact that previous twentieth-century efforts to develop national goals in education involved only professional educators. This may have been one of the factors contributing to the deep division between the educational establishment and the general public. This Commission has taken the position that if the reforms and programs described in this report are to be of practical value, goals must be developed in a participatory way, involving students, parents, and the general citizenry, as well as educators.

If educational goals are to be realized, they must form a frame of reference for student objectives. Objectives serve as indexes of the school's progress toward its goals. All participants in the educative process must know the goals and objectives of whatever they undertake. An awareness of the goals and objectives of their schools helps students establish personal goals and objectives and enables them to measure their individual progress.

The Commission does not advocate abandonment of the traditional high school. It does urge, however, that recognition be given to a wide variety of available alternatives. These alternatives offer a number of avenues by which learners may pursue secondary education based upon individual interests and objectives. It must be accepted that adolescents are no longer grown-up children nor are teachers walking encyclopedias. Today's student probably has in his head more raw information than teachers had thirty years ago.

In the years ahead, students whose needs are being adequately provided for will remain in traditional school environments. Students who are artistically inclined will learn in art museums, studios, and conservatories. Students who are skill-oriented will enter specific skill development centers or greatly expanded apprenticeship programs. Scientifically minded students will study in libraries, museums, zoos, and laboratories.

The provision of such alternatives will require changes in teacher preparation. Training institutions must prepare teachers to diagnose learning difficulties and prescribe appropriate experiences to overcome them. Those who train teachers have too often assumed that all students from middle- and upper-class backgrounds will be successful students. Teachers who have been prepared to teach middle-class children then prove inadequate when faced with children whose achievement is below average. This is a major reason why programs for low-income, low-achieving children have failed. They were instituted without sufficient diagnosis or concern for individual problems.

Toward Recommendations

No segment of education is an island. Implementation of the Commission's recommendations has implications beyond the reform of secondary education. What is possible at the secondary level is limited by what happens in elementary and middle schools, and in higher education.

The recommendations in this report evolved from careful scrutiny of the schools and long debate by the National Commission on the Reform of Secondary Education. Some of the recommendations may seem radical, but today's conditions must be treated at the roots.

NOTES

1. *A Foundation Goes to School* (New York: Ford Foundation, 1972), p. 3.

2. Paul Goodman, *Growing Up Absurd: Problems of Youth in Organized Society* (New York: Random House, 1956).

CHAPTER 2

Recommendations for Improving Secondary Education

The reform of secondary education cannot be accomplished by educators working alone. It requires the ingenuity and assistance of many people in the community served by a particular school. The recommendations of the Commission must be considered in this framework.

Recommendation No. 1: Defining Secondary School Expectations

Every secondary school and its subordinate departments must formulate a statement of goals and develop performance criteria for students. Goals and objectives should be published in information bulletins for students and parents and be posted in a conspicuous place within the school building.

Recommendation No. 2: Community Participation in Determining Secondary School Expectations

Schools will not be able to achieve their purposes without increased help from the people in the communities they serve.

Communities must participate in the formulation of goals and in continuing efforts to refine and adapt the statements of goals and objectives. The communities as a whole, not solely the subsection called schools, must achieve the goals.

Recommendation No. 3: The Basis for Curricular Revision

The high schools should no longer be required to perform purely custodial functions. Attempts to keep in school adolescents who do not wish to be there damage the environment for learning. The content of traditional high school curricula should be revised to eliminate busy-work components designed merely to occupy the time of adolescents who are in school only because the law requires it. Revitalization of the curriculum will require attention to the earlier maturation of adolescents. Intelligent evaluation of curricular revision must grow from valid measurements of the degree to which students are achieving the stated goals and objectives of their school.

Recommendation No. 4: Teacher Training

Teacher training institutions should revise their programs so that prospective teachers are exposed to the variety of teaching and learning options in secondary education. New teachers should be able to work in several instructional modes.

Extensive in-service programs should be instituted to retrain teachers presently employed to equip them with a greater variety of approaches and skills. This need will become increasingly acute as the decline in birth rate encumbers the schools with aging teaching staffs.

Recommendation No. 5: Bias in Textbooks

State legislatures must ensure that procedures are established so that textbooks and materials used in the schools do not present inaccurate accounts of the contributions of various ethnic groups or inaccurate portrayals of the role of women.

Recommendation No. 6: Bias in Counseling

Counselors should ensure that all students, regardless of sex or ethnic background, are afforded equal latitude and equally positive guidance in making educational choices.

Recommendation No. 7: Affirmative Action

Every high school should establish an affirmative action committee composed of students, former students, faculty, and community representatives. The purpose of this committee is to examine and report to the administration on instances of inequality and discrimination involving students or groups of students at the school.

Recommendation No. 8: Expanding Career Opportunities

Secondary schools must realign their curricula to provide students with a range of experiences and activities broad enough to permit them to take full advantage of career opportunities in their communities. To meet this objective, basic components of the school program will have to be offered in the late afternoon or in the evening for some students.

Recommendation No. 9: Career Education

Career education advisory councils including representatives of labor, business, community, students, and former students should be established to assist in planning and implementing career education programs in comprehensive high schools.

Career awareness programs should be initiated as an integral part of the curriculum to assure an appreciation of the dignity of work.

Opportunities for exploration in a variety of career clusters should be available to students in grades 8 through 10.

In grades 11 and 12, students should have opportunities to acquire hard skills in a career area of their choice. This training should involve experience in the world outside school and should equip the student with job-entry skills.

Recommendation No. 10: Job Placement

Suitable job placement must be an integral part of the career education program for students planning to enter the labor force upon leaving school. Secondary schools should establish an employment office staffed by career counselors and clerical assistants. The office should work in close cooperation with the state employment services. Agencies certifying counselors for secondary schools should require such counselors to show experience in job placement as a condition for granting initial certification.

Recommendation No. 11: Global Education

The education of the nation's adolescents must be superior to that of their parents. Part of this superiority must be an enhanced sense of the globe as the human environment, and instruction to this end must reflect not only the ancient characteristics of the world, but emerging knowledge of biological and social unity. All secondary school students should receive a basic global education.

New instructional material for global education must be prepared if this recommendation is to be effective. State departments of education should require teacher training institutions to design programs which prepare teachers to present such programs.

Recommendation No. 12: Alternative Paths to High School Completion

A wide variety of paths leading to completion of requirements for graduation from high school should be made available to all students. Individual students must be encouraged to assume major responsibilty for the determination of their educational goals, the development of the learning activities needed to achieve those goals, and the appraisal of their progress.

Recommendation No. 13: Local Board Responsibilities for Funding Alternatives

Whenever a student chooses an acceptable alternative to the comprehensive high school, local school boards should fund his education at the level of current expenditure computed for other students.

Recommendation No. 14: Credit for Experience

Secondary schools should establish extensive programs to award academic credit for accomplishment outside the building, and for learning that occurs on the job, whether the job be undertaken for pay, for love, or for its own sake. Community involvement will, of course, be required in such a program and should be as encompassing as possible.

Recommendation No. 15: Secondary Level Examination Program

The College Level Examination Board should expand its College Level Examination Program to include a comparable Secondary Level Examination Program. The tests should be routinely administered quarterly or monthly to help adolescents to obtain credit for work done outside the classroom.

Recommendation No. 16: Broadcast Television

Major funding sources, including both foundations and the National Institute of Education, should initiate and support extensive research into the influence of television on students' attitudes, perceptions, and life styles. The purpose of this research should be to suggest changes in school curricula and instructional approach.

The broadcasting industry should establish media fellowships designed to afford secondary school teachers and instructional leaders the opportunity to study the use of broadcast commercial television for educational purposes.

Recommendation No. 17: Classroom Use of Broadcast Material

Copyright laws and union contracts should be written to make sure that classroom use of broadcast materials copied off the air is not unnecessarily restricted. Television programs should never be asked to carry instructional burdens alone. Books and pamphlets must be specially and carefully prepared to accompany all instruction via television. Both the instructional television program and the printed materials should be available in public libraries as well as in schools.

Recommendation No. 18: Cable Television

When cable franchises are awarded, the local school system should have exclusive use of three channels during the daytime, with possible use of more as needed. At least one—and preferably all three—of these cable channels should continue to be available for nighttime viewing by school students or for purposes of adult education.

Recommendation No. 19: Flexibility of Alternative Programs

Differing time sequences—hourly, daily, weekly, yearly—must be made available so that educational programs can be adapted to the needs of individual students.

Schools are already moving away from the Carnegie Unit and are beginning to grant credit on the basis of competence, demonstrated experience, and a host of other assessments. It is recommended that this practice be expanded and that the Carnegie Unit become merely one of the alternative ways of granting credit.

Recommendation No. 20: Rank in Class

Articulation between secondary schools and post-secondary schools must be improved, with each level seeking to support the educational efforts of the other. Personnel representing both levels must cooperatively develop alternatives to grade-point average and rank in class for assessing the scope and quality of the education received by students at the secondary level. High schools should stop calculating student rank in class for any purpose.

Recommendation No. 21: Planning for School Security

All secondary school systems should develop security plans to safeguard students, faculty, equipment, and facilities. Specific procedures must be developed for faculty members to follow in case of disruption.

Recommendation No. 22: Records of Violence

State legislation should be enacted to require principals to file a detailed report on all serious assaults within schools. The information contained should form a data base from which security personnel could identify potential trouble areas and move to alleviate future problems.

Recommendation No. 23: Code of Student Rights and Obligations

Every secondary school should develop and adopt a code of student rights and obligations. This code should be published and distributed to every student. It should include all school rules, regulations, and procedures for suspension and expulsion with explanations of how students can defend themselves through established process.

Recommendation No. 24: School Newspapers

A school newspaper is a house organ which is operated, financed, and therefore controlled by the school system, which may be legally liable for its contents. In cases where students and school administrators become deadlocked over censorship, a student-faculty-community committee should decide the issue. Some schools may find it necessary to withdraw financial support, allowing students complete freedom of expression in what would then be entirely their own publication, with a corresponding liability for what is printed.

Recommendation No. 25: Right of Privacy

A student's school records must contain only factual information necessary to the educative process. The entire file must be available at all times for review by students and their parents but must not be accessible to "persons not in interest." Records should be forwarded to another school system, university, or prospective employer only at the written request of the student, his parents, or the receiving school.

That part of a student's records which pertain to his mental health should contain only entries made under the direction of the student's physician and must be kept separately from his academic records. The complete record or any of its contents should be released only to the student, his parents, or to his physician at the student's or parent's request.

Recommendation No. 26: Corporal Punishment

Several states have outlawed corporal punishment with no resulting loss in control or authority. Corporal punishment should be abolished by statute in all states. In the modern world, corporal punishment is necessarily "cruel and unusual."

Recommendation No. 27: Student Activities

Scholarship should not be a requisite for participation in sports, band, singing, cheerleading, or other student activities important to the social development of adolescents. Neither the local school nor state activities associations should establish scholarship standards. Any student in good standing in a school should have the right to participate in any of the school's activities with the exception of honor societies specifically established to reward scholarship.

Recommendation No. 28: Compulsory Attendance

If the high school is not to be a custodial institution, the state must not force adolescents to attend. Earlier maturity—physical, sexual, and intellectual—requires an option of earlier departure from the restraints of formal schooling.

The formal school-leaving age should be dropped to age fourteen. Other programs should accommodate those who wish to leave school, and employment laws should be rewritten to assure on-the-job training in full-time service and work.

Recommendation No. 29: Free K–14 Public Education

The Congress of the United States in conjunction with state legislatures should enact legislation that will entitle each citizen to fourteen years of tuition-free education beyond kindergarten, only eight of which would be compulsory. The remaining six years should be available for use by anyone at any stage of his life. Congressional involvement is essential to assure equal access in an age of interstate mobility.

Recommendation No. 30: Youth Organizations

The National Association of Secondary School Principals, a professional organization for school administrators, currently operates two of the largest organizations affecting public high school youth: the National Student Council Association and the National Honor Society. The principals' group should dissociate itself from these organizations and help them become independent national youth organizations.

Recommendation No. 31: Sexism

School administrators and school boards, at both the state and local levels, must set forth commitments to eliminate all vestiges of sexism in the schools.

Areas of immediate concern are equal employment and treatment of the sexes in instructional and administrative positions, equal opportunities for female students to participate in all curricula areas, including career education, and the elimination of all courses required of only one sex.

Individual teachers should make sure they are not focusing their teaching toward either sex.

All female students who become pregnant should be permitted to remain in school for the full term of pregnancy if they wish to do so and their physician considers it feasible. They should be permitted to return to school following childbirth as soon as released by their physician. There must be no denial of the right to participate in activities because of pregnancy or motherhood, whether the girl is wed or unwed.

Recommendation No. 32: Females in Competitive Team Sports

School boards and administrators at the local level must provide opportunities for female students to participate in programs of competitive team sports that are comparable to the opportunities for males. The programs must be adequately funded through regular school budgets.

Outstanding female athletes must not be excluded from competition as members of male teams in noncontact sports. The fact that a school offers the same team sport for girls should not foreclose this option.

State activities associations should be required by statute to eliminate from their constitutions and bylaws all constraints to full participation in competitive team sports by females.

If state activities associations are to continue to have jurisdiction over female sports, they should be required by state statute to have equal sex representation on all boards supervising boys' and girls' athletics.

PART II

NEW
NATIONAL
GOALS

CHAPTER 3

National Goals of Education

Recommendation No. 1: Defining Secondary School Expectations

Every secondary school and its subordinate departments must formulate a statement of goals and develop performance criteria for students. Goals and objectives should be published in information bulletins for students and parents and be posted in a conspicuous place within the school building.

Recommendation No. 2: Community Participation in Determining Secondary School Expectations

Schools will not be able to achieve their purposes without increased help from the people in the communities they serve. Communities must participate in the formulation of goals and in continuing efforts to refine and adapt the statements of goals and objectives. The communities as a whole, not solely the subsection called schools, must achieve the goals.

The Need for Goals

The ultimate purpose of public secondary schools and school systems in America is to provide educational opportunities to

25

satisfy both the common and the unique needs of the individuals who aggregate to the total population. Public secondary schools are responsible for delivering a quality education to all youth. Quality education with reference to common needs implies the ability to perform basic skills at a level commensurate with ability. With reference to unique needs, quality education implies development of specific knowledge and skills to the level of proficiency required for success in future endeavors.

To accomplish this mission, a school must diagnose each learner's needs, concerns, and cognitive and affective styles, and cut its cloth to fit each design. The compensatory approach and all other efforts to equalize educational opportunity have produced entirely unsatisfactory results, and nothing now remains but thoroughgoing reform of secondary education.

The Commission believes that its list of suggested national goals for secondary education represents a point of departure for reform. The proposed goals provide a framework for educational experiences that will enable people of great diversity to live together in harmony while maintaining their individuality; to employ critical analysis to the solution of problems presented by rapid change; and to value continuous learning as a means of satisfactory adjustment. The goals provide a strategy for developing effective oral and written communication as well as for providing experiences which are thought-provoking, instructive, and self-fulfilling.

The purpose of goals is to indicate the direction in which the schools should be moving. If goals are to be realized, methods of assessing the accomplishment of objectives must be formulated as points along the way. State departments of education, school boards, and schools must develop these methods within the framework of goals. The indexes must be precisely defined in order to measure the success of secondary schools in reaching toward these goals and to point the way for further change.

The central purposes of secondary education should be frequently examined and set forth as a statement of long-range goals. They should be readily available to everyone engaged in the process of teaching and learning and frequently discussed.

Because American schools serve the needs of society, the purposes of education must be modified as society changes. If educational goals are to be of practical value, they cannot clash with the realities of a changing economic and social situation. They must be developed in a participatory way with input from students, parents, and the general citizenry. The values which legitimize educational goals are the product of experience, and to a degree they change with experience. If the schools are to be responsive to society, educational goals must be reconstituted periodically.

Unfortunately, people grow accustomed to goals: they are part of the furniture. Goals for education, once established, tend to be taken for granted and handed down from generation to generation, just as the school buildings are passed on from one age to another.

In the twentieth century, three significant efforts have been made to state appropriate goals for the nation's secondary schools. Each of these past endeavors was undertaken by groups of professional educators. In the seventies, the role of educators must be participatory only, and the setting of goals must involve all the citizenry.

The first and foremost of the efforts to define the purposes of secondary education was that of the Commission on the Reorganization of Secondary Education in 1918. The summary statement of this commission, sponsored by the National Education Association, enunciated the following goals for secondary education: (1) health, (2) command of fundamental processes, (3) worthy home membership, (4) vocation, (5) citizenship, (6) worthy use of leisure time, and (7) ethical character. These became widely known as the Seven Cardinal Principles of Secondary Education.[1]

The second twentieth-century definition of the purposes of secondary education was expressed in 1938 by the Education Policies Commission of the National Education Association and the American Association of School Administrators. The group developed a number of goals under four headings: (1) self-realization, (2) human relationships, (3) economic efficiency, and (4) civic responsibility.[2]

A third endeavor to set goals for education was made by the President's Commission on National Goals, which was appointed by President Eisenhower and which made its report on November 16, 1960. The most applicable new goal for the high school was expressed succinctly: "It is essential that the tradition of the comprehensive high school should be preserved and strengthened."[3]

The education section of the Eisenhower Commission report, of course, was written in the shadow of James Bryant Conant's recently published (1959) and very influential study, *The American High School Today*, which had been sponsored by the Carnegie Corporation. The general theme of the Conant report had been that the nation needed more and better comprehensive high schools, with better programs for the gifted in a comprehensive nexus.

By far the most significant of these historical efforts was the set of Seven Cardinal Principles. In many ways, these were not goals but eternal verities. Perhaps this is why they have been able to sustain a lasting commitment from the educational profession.

As late as 1966, the Research Division of the National Education Association polled a sample of the teaching profession on the appropriateness of the Seven Cardinal Principles as current goals. The question was, "Is this a satisfactory list of the major goals of education today as you would see them?" More than 85 percent of the teachers polled responded, "Yes."

The equally strong commitment of administrators to these fifty-five-year-old principles was expressed by a principal who recently responded as follows to an inquiry from this Commission: "Your question about national goals for secondary schools at first seemed quite simple, as most educators believe that this was answered for all time with the formulation of the Cardinal Principles so many years ago."[4]

In proclaiming the Seven Cardinal Principles, however, the Commission on the Reorganization of Secondary Education did not attempt to set them in concrete. The introduction to the commission report reads as follows:

> Secondary education should be determined by the needs of the society to be served, the character of the individuals to be educated, and the knowledge of educational theory and practice available. These factors are by no means static. Society is always in process of development; the character of the secondary-school population undergoes modification; and the sciences on which educational theory and practice depend constantly furnish new information. Secondary education, however, like any other established agency of society, is conservative and tends to resist modification. Failure to make adjustments when the need arises leads to the necessity for extensive reorganization at irregular intervals.[5]

The time for "extensive reorganization" of secondary education is again at hand.

Need for New Goals

In the fifty-five years since the announcement of the Seven Cardinal Principles the population of the United States has doubled, and a nation that was approximately one-half rural has become approximately four-fifths urban. The national income in constant prices is six times as high today as it was then. There are seven times as many students in high school and, in order of magnitude, more automobiles. At the time of the Cardinal Principles, *Plessy v. Ferguson*—separate but equal—was good law; what desegregation in the federal service had been achieved under Theodore Roosevelt and Taft had been reversed by the Wilson administration. One need look no further than the Cardinal Principle which calls for girls only to receive training in home economics to realize how completely inappropriate goals from the 1910s must be for the schools of the 1970s. It is past time for national goals that will give the schools a new alignment to the needs of society.

The need for goals and the distinction between goals and objectives were succinctly stated by former Commissioner of Education Sterling McMurrin:

> *Goals,* carefully conceived and formulated, indicate the purposes of institutions and the directions in which they intend to move. Goals should be few in number. Objectives, which must change with changing circumstances, are points along the way which must be reached if the basic goals are to be realized. Objectives must be concrete and specific to facilitate the making of decisions, whether those decisions concern the appointment of faculty, the admission of students, the development of curricula, or the allocation of financial resources.[6]

Many individual states, districts, and schools have recently proclaimed statements of goals, but no extensive effort has been made to unify these approaches. The consequence is that little or no agreement exists on a nationwide basis as to what the purpose and direction of secondary education should be. But the existence of these many recent attempts has eased the work of this Commission.

The Procedure

The goals of the Commission were developed through the following process:

The professional staff of the Commission analyzed the recently announced goals of thirty-seven individual states,* along

* In almost every case, the state goals were developed by committees made up of citizens, legislators, and educators.

with the compilation of state goals prepared by the Cooperative Accountability Project of Denver, Colorado.[7] A list of
goals was made on the basis of frequency of appearance in the
state documents. This list of goals was submitted to Dr.
George Gallup of Gallup International, who restated them for
purposes of public opinion research.

Utilizing the Gallup survey procedure, the professional staff
submitted questionnaires to panels of superintendents, principals, teachers, parents, and students representing a mix of
urban, suburban, and rural populations. The purpose of the
surveys was to substantiate the relevance of the goals adopted
by the states. The use of parents and students assured the
Commission of verification from persons other than educators.

The results of the national goals surveys are presented in
Appendix A. There is very little disagreement among the four
groups polled on the desirability of the goals, the responsibility of the schools for achieving them, or the levels of success
of recent graduates. Parents, much more than anyone in the
schools, regard computation skills as "essential"; teachers,
much less than any of the others, regard occupational competence as essential; parents and students are less likely than
the others to say that "knowledge of self" and "appreciation
of others" are responsibilities of the schools. But even in this
area, agreement is more common than disagreement.

The Nature of Goals

The goals of secondary education are the long-range results
which society expects its secondary schools to accomplish. The
goals can be divided into categories of content and process.

Content goals are the general skills that students must acquire if they are to function at a level that is both personally
and socially rewarding.

Process goals are the individual abilities and attitudes which are influenced by the procedures, environment, and activities of the school.

The goals suggested by this Commission are learner-centered. The responsibility for achieving these goals rests with teachers, administrators, school board members, parents, and, to a very considerable degree, the students themselves.

Goals for Secondary Education

CONTENT GOALS

· *Achievement of Communication Skills.* The secondary school must ensure that every student masters the basic skills of reading, writing, speaking, listening, and viewing. Mastery should be acquired through a wide variety of appropriate experiences and activities in each of the skills areas. The high school has an obligation to certify that every graduate has mastered the skills of reading and writing to a level of functional literacy.

· *Achievement of Computation Skills.* The secondary school is obliged to ensure that all students master those computational and analytical skills necessary for the understanding of everyday problems. The high school has an obligation to certify that every graduate has mastered the skills of computation to a level sufficient for the management of household responsibilities.

· *Attainment of Proficiency in Critical and Objective Thinking.* The secondary school is obliged to ensure that all learners develop, to the extent of their abilities, the skills of critical and objective thinking through research, analysis, and evaluation.

· *Acquisition of Occupational Competence.* The secondary school must seek to prepare students for a successful life of work through increasing their occupational options. It must ensure that those students who wish to do so acquire job-entry skills before leaving high school. This effort must be coupled with employment opportunities, which are the responsibility of the society as a whole.

• *Clear Perception of Nature and Environment.* The secondary school must equip all students· with an understanding of the wonders of nature, of the effects of man upon his environment, and of man's obligations to the viability of the planet.

• *Development of Economic Understanding.* The secondary school is obliged to help students understand the American economy, its accomplishments, and its relationship to individual rights and freedoms. Each learner should understand his role in the economy as both producer and consumer of goods and services.

• *Acceptance of Responsibility for Citizenship.* The secondary school must help students understand the American system of government, and equip them with the knowledge and experiences necessary for dealing purposefully with the political process. Citizenship responsibilities include respect for the opinions of others, the ability to conduct rational and informed discussions of controversial issues, respect for public and private property, and the acceptance of social duties.

PROCESS GOALS

• *Knowledge of Self.* The secondary school is obliged to assist every learner in assessing his/her own mental, physical, and emotional capacities to the end that he/she has a positive self-image and can cope with problems of personal and family management. Schools also have an obligation to help learners understand their own physical nature and the extent to which their subsequent potential may be affected by their habits in eating and drinking and use of leisure time.

• *Appreciation of Others.* The secondary school must

help each student develop an understanding of the differences and similarities and of the common humanity of members of different ethnic and religious groups.

• *Ability to Adjust to Change.* The secondary school must endow students with the knowledge and attitudes necessary for survival in the twenty-first century and for coping with the unprecedented expansion of knowledge.

• *Respect for Law and Authority.* The secondary school is obliged to seek to develop within each student a respect for duly constituted authority and public laws as well as a knowledge of the strategy for changing both through the democratic process.

• *Clarification of Values.* The secondary school must assist each learner in developing increased awareness of himself and of his relations to others and to the universe as he seeks to discover values and ethical standards which can promote growth toward his highest potential.

• *Appreciation of the Achievements of Man.* The secondary school is obliged to help students understand and appreciate man's historical achievements in art, music, drama, literature, and the sciences so that they may acquire reverence for the heritage of mankind.

Continuous versus Changing Goals

The Cardinal Principles of the Commission on the Reorganization of Secondary Education were laid down at a time of great expansion of secondary education and of belief in what it could accomplish. The national goals here proposed by the Commission on the Reform of Secondary Education are written at a time when the nation must expect a reduction in the size of its secondary system and feels diminished beliefs in its capabilities. Both the similarities and disparities of the goals themselves are worthy of note.

Both commissions concur on the importance of basic skills

in the areas of communication and computation. They both call for an understanding of citizenship responsibilities, with this Commission broadening the concept into three goals rather than one. The need for occupational competence is expressed by both commissions.

The worthy use of leisure time was seen as an enduring need by the commission of 1918. The Commission of the 1970s, on the other hand, takes the position that rewarding use of leisure would be a natural outcome if all other goals were successfully met. Health is a goal of both commissions; but while the earlier one stressed physical fitness, today's Commission is also concerned with a student's mental and emotional needs and adjustment to the unprecedented acceleration of change.

In general, the authors of the Cardinal Principles regarded students as big children, while the authors of the new goals consider them young adults. The new Commission also treats the sexes equally in responsibilities and potential. Other concerns of the seventies which were not issues in 1918 are expressed in the Secondary Reform Commission's goals on economic understanding, nature and environment, and the appreciation of others.

A graphic comparison of the differences between the 1918 Seven Cardinal Principles and the 1973 Goals for Secondary Education appears as Appendix B.

Who Develops Goals?

In the past, the development of goals for education has been considered the exclusive province of educators. In the seventies, society's concern with schools makes the role of the educator no more than participatory.

Society must take secondary education much more seriously than it has in the past. If the institutions which serve the nation's adolescents at this crucial point in their development are to perform their missions, they must have the continuing interest and support of the public. Secondary schools can serve society only when the citizenry plays a deliberate part in setting the goals of education.

NOTES

1. *Cardinal Principles of Secondary Education*, Bureau of Education Bulletin No. 35 (Washington, D.C.: Government Printing Office, 1918).

2. Education Policies Commission, *The Purposes of Education in American Democracy* (Washington, D.C.: National Education Association and American Association of School Administrators, 1938), p. 157.

3. President's Commission on National Goals, *Goals for Americans* (New York: The American Assembly, 1960), p. 85.

4. Letter of response to the National Commission on the Reform of Secondary Education from Mr. Robert E. Bruton, principal of Merritt Island High School, Merritt Island, Fla., Sept. 13, 1972.

5. *Cardinal Principles of Secondary Education*, p. 7.

6. Academy for Educational Development, *Management Forum*, vol. 1, no. 2, p. 1, Washington, D.C., October 1972.

7. Hanson P. Gordon, *State Goals for Elementary and Secondary Education* (Denver, Colo.: Cooperative Accountability Project, 1972).

PART III

REVITALIZING THE CONTENT OF SECONDARY EDUCATION

CHAPTER 4

Emerging Components of Secondary School Reform

Recommendation No. 3: The Basis for Curricular Revision

The high schools should no longer be required to perform purely custodial functions. Attempts to keep in school adolescents who do not wish to be there damage the environment for learning. The content of traditional high school curricula should be revised to eliminate busy-work components designed merely to occupy the time of adolescents who are in school only because the law requires it. Revitalization of the curriculum will require attention to the earlier maturation of adolescents. Intelligent evaluation of curricular revision must grow from valid measurements of the degree to which students are achieving the stated goals and objectives of their school.

Recommendation No. 4: Teacher Training

Teacher training institutions should revise their programs so that prospective teachers are exposed to the variety of teach-

ing and learning options in secondary education. New teachers should be able to work in several instructional modes.

Extensive in-service programs should be instituted to retrain teachers presently employed to equip them with a greater variety of approaches and skills. This need will become increasingly acute as the decline in birth rate encumbers the schools with aging teaching staffs.

Recommendation No. 5: Bias in Textbooks

State legislatures must ensure that procedures are established so that textbooks and materials used in the schools do not present inaccurate accounts of the contributions of various ethnic groups or inaccurate portrayals of the role of women.

Recommendation No. 6: Bias in Counseling

Counselors should ensure that all students, regardless of sex or ethnic background, are afforded equal latitude and equally positive guidance in making educational choices.

Recommendation No. 7: Affirmative Action

Every high school should establish an affirmative action committee composed of students, former students, faculty, and community representatives. The purpose of this committee is to examine and report to the administration on instances of inequality and discrimination involving students or groups of students at the school.

The Commission has defined the goals of secondary education as the long-range results society expects its secondary schools to accomplish. To get there will require significant changes in course content, materials and methods of instruction, and organization of schools. The schools must keep up with the world around them.

The Content of Secondary Education

Planning for the content of secondary education has been a fragmented process which too often has reflected the com-

peting concerns of subject areas. The result has been the per-
petuation of programs and subject areas whose retention has
been rationalized as traditional or as "needed" to meet college
entrance requirements. The reform of secondary education
will be meaningless unless the focus of change in content
becomes the needs of students rather than the desires and
interests of competing members of high school staffs.

Today's schools must come to terms with the earlier maturation of students, both sexual and physical. The mean age at
which girls reach menarche seems to have been declining
steadily for at least a century. Voice change in boys, which
occurred at an average age of eighteen in the eighteenth
century, is now occurring at an average age of 13.3 years.
Some researchers have found a parallel acceleration in mental
development. Correlations have been reported between increased stature and higher mental test scores.[1] Such phenomena have wide social and educational implications; schools
cannot ignore them.

SCHOOLS AS CUSTODIAL INSTITUTIONS

Institutions that care for younger children offer a more
custodial service than those that care for older children. If
adolescents of this generation are "older" than those of previous generations, the schools must show it. The high school
calculus course need not require 180 hours in class if the
college course requires only 48 hours to cover the same material. In many cases a high school student may require more
than 180 hours in class even though the college course requires
only 48 hours to cover the same material. If we believe that
education should be individualized, it must be tailored to the
individual. It is hard to avoid the suspicion that the reasoning
behind all the hours that must be spent in the classroom is a
custodial logic.

Keeping adolescents off the street is in any event a function
the schools are not performing very well. The attempt to do
so is harmful to the learning environment. By the age of four-

teen, a student who has not developed some motivation toward learning is not likely to profit from compulsory schooling.

Secondary education must drop its custodial burdens and present its content in ways more consonant with the increasing maturity of students and the increasing depth and complexity of knowledge.

The National Assessment of Educational Progress

The National Assessment project, which was initiated in 1967 with loud expressions of alarm from the professional educators, has now matured to the point where its findings can contribute significantly to the reform of secondary school curricula. The National Assessment project is now sponsored by the Education Commission of the States, a group of state political leaders and school officers. Its purpose is to measure the results of American education by means of criterion-referenced tests administered to large samples of the population at different age levels. To date, the National Assessment project has produced reports on the achievement of minimal skills and understandings in six major curricular areas: science, writing, citizenship, reading, literature, and social studies. Several subjects are tested each year, and most are now in a second cycle to provide comparative data. The program, which measures how well students as a group achieve desirable goals, or a similar program, represents a point of beginning for school systems and schools.

Results of National Assessment findings are presented by age groups, size and type of community, sex, race, educational level of a parent, and by the four regions of the country. These analyses show a general inferiority of performance in the Southeast section of the country, in the extreme inner city, in rural areas, and among students whose parents have little formal education.

Many of the findings of the Assessment project can be used

to develop specific content revision. Assessments in the area of social studies, for example, indicate that high school students know much less about the structure and functions of local and state governments than they do about the national government. Seventeen-year-olds do not know how to influence local and state governments, the function or even the names of significant local officials. Since the eighteen-year-olds are now voting, and there is a national emphasis on decentralization and increased community participation, the National Assessment data offer a cue for drastic content revisions in social studies.

The observations of this Commission and the experiences of its members confirm reasons for dissatisfaction in the teaching of social studies. This unhappiness is not a new phenomenon. James Bryant Conant reported from his three-year study of the high school: "I found widespread dissatisfaction with the course in world history. Furthermore, I found few teachers or administrators who were willing to endorse a four-year sequence in social studies because of their doubts as to the value of what would be taught the fourth year." Members of this Commission noted that dissatisfaction with the teaching of world history continues and may even be greater than it was in 1959 when Conant made his study.

There is also increasing disenchantment with the way the teaching of American history is organized, and with state requirements that mandate three years of what is usually a narrowly nationalistic study. Americans already live in a highly interdependent world, and their children will have to live on much closer terms with the citizens of other countries. Without losing the values of cultural and historical identification, secondary education must present a more global view of the United States.

National Assessment findings in science argue that students understand the biological sciences much better than they do the physical sciences. An examination of existing curricula indicates that much more emphasis is placed on the biological sciences than on the physical sciences, largely because science teachers are more likely to be competent in the biological sciences. Eliminating these deficiencies is a task for the colleges and the teacher training institutions.

Results of the science tests show girls inferior to boys in science achievement, though they are superior in achievement in all the other five areas which have been assessed. The argument that this weakness in female education reflects a cultural bias in the larger society cannot stand unchallenged, for this is an area where the schools can influence the society.

Perhaps the most distressing finding in the National Assessment reports is the low level of competency in the mechanics of writing at every age level. The evidence mandates increased emphasis on these skills, even at some cost from reduced emphasis on the teaching of literature.

The National Assessment of Educational Progress should become the bulwark of educational accountability. Local educators should be equipped to compare realistically the achievement of their students with regional and national results. The findings of National Assessment should lead to various content revisions, curriculum reform, in-service efforts, and improved competency-based instruction.

Performance-Based Instruction

Beyond the primary level, education has always lacked precise objectives. Performance-based instruction seeks to remedy this flaw by specifying detailed objectives before teaching begins.

Performance-based instruction sets four essential conditions for the teacher's work. First, the teacher must target the results of the sets of contrived experiences he will direct, in terms of what he wishes the student to achieve. Second, he must describe each target in such a way that the student can measure his own success. Third, he must provide instruction that relates to the achievement of the target and that can be modified with reference to the student's progress. Finally, the entire system must be held accountable for each student. If the student does not succeed, the system, its components, and its interaction with other systems must be examined and altered until the target is achieved.

Targeting is the sine qua non of performance-based instruction. Once the target is known, the student can help himself. Instruction can be individualized; its quality can be assessed and improved. A basis can be established for the use of modern technological and managerial support services in the teaching process.

The Commission would like to say that performance-based instruction is upon us, but can find no evidence that it is. To date, few schools have actually instituted such programs. Nevertheless, there is reason to hope that as teachers write, revise, and rewrite the statements of objectives required by this approach to education, they will acquire the skills it demands.

The performance-based idea can imply any kind of teaching, from lecturing to computer-assisted instruction. If the targets are important and wide-ranging, if performance criteria are valid, if the measurement of results is reliable, and if system accountability is practiced, a performance base for instruction can lead to a more productive secondary school system.

Pluralism in Secondary Schools

The high schools have passed through a decade of social unrest, and have now learned the need for affirmative action, for using rather than opposing the variety of life styles in the mix of racial, religious, and ethnic groups who live together in America. But, there is still a lot to be done.

BIAS IN TEXTBOOKS

Discrimination against females, minorities, and the blue-collar working class is omnipresent in American textbooks, from the first primers in elementary school through the end of secondary education. Until recently, blacks and other minorities simply did not appear in elementary texts. Portrayals of families almost always showed a white, middle-class household with the father departing or returning home, dressed in business suit and carrying a briefcase; the mother was prettily dressed in attire suitable for social visits, sending or driving the children off to school.

Girls were usually shown as passive creatures with restricted body movements and limited facial expressions. Their activities were usually those associated with female functions within the home, while their male counterparts participated in exciting events with their fathers.

At the secondary level, the contributions of blacks, other minorities, and women were excluded from the pages of history books. These omissions implied that during the nation's developmental periods, the country was inhabited entirely by white, Anglo-Saxon males, and that the roles of blacks, other minorities, and women were unimportant.

Instructional materials dealing with careers and occupations also lack portrayals of members of minority groups. Women are usually shown as secretaries, nurses, elementary school teachers, airline stewardesses, and so on.

Strong action is required at the legislative and state department of education levels to resolve the problem of bias in textbooks. Publishers of textbooks are slow to change, especially when a book is widely used. Positive and persistent pressure must be applied to correct sexist discrepancies in textbooks and other materials used in teachnig and learning.

COUNSELING IN A PLURALISTIC ENVIRONMENT

Various groups promoting the interests of minorities and women report that the attitudes of high school counselors have serious effects upon the quality and practicality of the education sought by girls and by students from minority groups. Counselors' attitudes and practices often discourage their hopes, limit their senses of autonomy, and damage their self-images.

Females are counseled against pursuing advanced courses in mathematics and science and are not encouraged to train for careers which have been dominated by males. Minority students are often counseled into areas of vocational training which lead to dead ends, and even to trades where they cannot sell the skills they have acquired.

Counselors must recognize their responsibility for today's low enrollment of girls in science and mathematics courses in the high schools, and for the unambitious programs offered to and the inadequate demands made upon students from minority groups. Counselors must also recognize an obligation to correct these discriminatory attitudes when they advise tomorrow's students.

PLURALISTIC INTERESTS AND VALUES

Cultural and ethnic groups are struggling against the homogenizing influences of technology, the mass media, and desegregation, hoping to retain meaningful identities and values from diverse ancestries. Historically, the schools have opposed such efforts at cultural separateness, espousing the doctrine of the melting pot. Now they are called upon to help groups maintain their sense of individual identity.

It will not be easy for an aging teaching staff to cope with the problems of prejudice and habit. The solution calls for: (1) a more careful and thoughtful insistence that ethnic groups respect one another, (2) the ability to recognize, evaluate, and settle value conflicts when they arise in the classroom and in the school, and (3) a new emphasis on the appreciation of diverse values.

Emphasis on the appreciation of diverse values cannot be limited to purely social or humanistic values. This country from the days of the Founding Fathers has had a deeply ingrained religious sense. Appreciation of diverse values must include, as well, appreciation of the diverse religious values which this nation has always encouraged and treasured.

Certainly every school must work with its students to help them in the development of a basic code of ethics and in providing them with a climate where a sense of moral development founded on the virtue of justice, if not love, becomes desirable.

NOTE

1. "Boys and Girls Are Now Maturing Earlier," *The New York Times,* Jan. 24, 1971, p. 1, col. 4.

CHAPTER 5

Career Education
as Part of the Curriculum

Recommendation No. 8: Expanding Career Opportunities

Secondary schools must realign their curricula to provide students with a range of experience and activities broad enough to permit them to take full advantage of career opportunities in their communities. To meet this objective, basic components of the school program will have to be offered in the late afternoon or in the evening for some students.

Recommendation No. 9: Career Education

Career education advisory councils including representatives of labor, business, community, students, and former students should be established to assist in planning and implementing career education programs in comprehensive high schools.

Career awareness programs should be initiated as an integral part of the curriculum to assure an appreciation of the dignity of work.

Opportunities for exploration in a variety of career clusters should be available to students in grades 8 through 10.

In grades 11 and 12, students should have opportunities to acquire hard skills in a career area of their choice. This training should involve experience in the world outside school and should equip the student with job-entry skills.

Recommendation No. 10: Job Placement

Suitable job placement must be an integral part of the career education program for students planning to enter the labor force upon leaving school. Secondary schools should establish an employment office staffed by career counselors and clerical assistants. The office should work in close co-operation with the state employment services. Agencies certifying counselors for secondary schools should require such counselors to show experience in job placement as a condition for granting initial certification.

In the American system of secondary education, "work" is a four-letter word. Far too many teachers and principals are not even sure it has redeeming social value outside the academic professions. Though the announced national commitment to vocational education goes back to the early part of the century, most programs are inconsequential. In comprehensive high schools, the vocational "track" is often worse than inconsequential.

The dilemma has historical and psychological causes. In their formative years, American high schools were organized to serve a select group of students who were beginning their training for a professional career. When the schools began to expand, late in the nineteenth century, the first of all commissions on educational reform, chaired by Charles W. Eliot of Harvard, insisted on the maintenance of a classical education. It was the failure of this classical program that called forth the commission which wrote the Cardinal Principles. But, in 1918 skilled trades were still communicated through apprenticeship, and the idea of extensive training for job-entry was foreign to most educators. It has never been entirely domesticated. Education for leisure still looms larger than education for work; education for going-on-to-college is so much bigger it is overwhelming.

In its first annual report, published in 1969, the National Advisory Council on Vocational Education pinpoints the psychology:

> At the very heart of our problem is a national attitude that says vocational education is designed for somebody else's children. This attitude is shared by businessmen, labor leaders, administrators, teachers, parents, and students. We are all guilty. We have promoted the idea that the only good education is an education capped by four years of college. This idea, transmitted by our values, our aspirations, and our silent support, is snobbish, undemocratic, and a revelation of why schools fail so many students. . . .[1]

A nationally prominent school superintendent expressed the issue very clearly in a report to the commission on the status of vocational education:

> The nation must change the value that it places on employment-oriented education. The aspect of our secondary program which is most damaging to young people is the stigma that we have attached to employment-oriented education. Everyone agrees that vocational education is extremely important. It receives top priority so long as it is for our neighbor's child rather than our own. If we are going to help our young people to learn how to catch their own fish rather than to line up at the welfare cafeteria for handout filets, then we must change the value which we place on employment-oriented education.[2]

John Gardner once wrote that a society which honors its philosophers but not its plumbers will shortly find that neither its philosophy nor its pipes will hold water. It could be argued that America is already far advanced toward that sorry condition. To reverse these trends, the schools must accept as a major objective a significant improvement of the reputation and the curricula of vocational training.

A national objective of great importance is the upgrading and expansion of occupational education for all, until all secondary school students who wish to do so can leave high school equipped with marketable skills whether or not they plan to continue their education.

The U.S. Office of Education Approach

Unfortunately, the simple necessity for greater concentration on vocational education is now being confused by the U.S. Office of Education's broad-brush plans for career education. The career education program proposed by the Office is highly theoretical, and the probability of its implementation as presently designed is approximately zero.

Dr. James D. Koerner, program director of the Alfred P. Sloan Foundation, has investigated the implications of the current USOE proposal for Career Education, and reported his findings to the Commission:

> Career Education, as proposed by the United States Office of Education, contemplates nothing less than a revolution. Every syllabus curriculum guide has to be conceived anew. Every teacher and administrator (both elementary and secondary) has to be retrained and educated. In short, every activity of every school will have to be replanned around what is called the world of work.

Dr. Koerner's analysis is documented by the following official definition of career education from the U.S. Department of Health, Education, and Welfare: "The fundamental concept of career education is that all educational experiences, curriculum, instruction, and counseling should be geared to preparation for economic independence and an appreciation for the dignity of work."[3]

This Commission, like the Office of Education, is deeply

concerned about the number of young people leaving school without marketable skills, the growing ranks of the unemployed, the number of persons entering the labor force in jobs very different from those they were prepared for, and the increasing number of persons who are unhappy in their present employment. It is also committed to a concept of career education as a phase of educational reform.

The Commission's concept and program for career education, however, can be immediately implemented by most secondary school districts. It does not look for "pie in the sky" but for "bread on the table."

Perhaps the major difference between the Office of Education's position on career education and the Commission's position is that the Commission does not believe that all educational experiences should be geared to preparation for making a living. A great deal of learning should be centered around personal satisfaction and pleasure. In brief, education should be geared not only to man's work, but also to his leisure.

The Post–High School Dropout Problem

Wide support is building in the Congress for a plan to give all secondary students training that guarantees them marketable skills. The strongest argument in support of this reform is the post–high school dropout problem. This situation is now so serious that "of the more than one million young people who enter college each year, fewer than half will complete two years of study, and only about one-third will ever complete a four-year course of study."[4]

Former U.S. Representative Roman Pucinski, the architect of the Vocational Education Amendments of 1968, described this alarming situation to the Commission:

The most serious social problem of today is not the high school dropout but the college dropout. Here is a youngster who has been very carefully prepared for 12 years to go to college. He's totally oblivious to the world of work. He has no job skills, doesn't know how to go about looking for a job, has no concept of what it means to be looking for a job, because he has been carefully prepared to go to college. . . .

In my judgment, the potential college dropout could be helped substantially by a career component in education, simply because he would have a fall-back position along with the high school dropout. If you give all youngsters career education, I feel you would psychologically prepare them. If their plans don't work out, then they have a fall-back position. They have the emotional and psychological security of knowing that they have an ace up their sleeve if everything else fails. I think career education would be a big help in that situation.[5]

The emotional trauma experienced by such large numbers of students creates an urgent need for broadening career education curricula to include all secondary school students. High school curricula should be expanded so that all adolescents can participate in cooperative work-study programs while pursuing other educational interests. The traditional barriers between vocational and academic "tracks" must be eliminated to permit students to cross lines in pursuit of their individual educational goals. All options must remain open as long as possible to all students.

The model for an expansion of career curricula is the Diversified Cooperative Training Program, which traditionally allows work-study opportunities to a limited number of students. The Commission's proposal is much broader than the DCT program. For example, many state plans for DCT require that a student work a minimum of 540 hours to obtain two school credits. The Commission proposes that credit be granted on the basis of student accomplishment rather than clock hours on the job. It proposes an academic umbrella under which every type of work in the community is available as a training program for high school students.

In the Commission's preferred plan, businesses will pay the students for apprenticeship. Where businesses are unwilling to pay, the schools must fund the program themselves, contracting with employers for the necessary services. The basic element in the Commission's proposal is the revitalization of apprenticeship as the best strategy for learning about work.

Career Education—A Matter of Urgency

Adolescents who need career education cannot await the outcome of Congressional debate over funding a new national program. The schools must make a start themselves, especially in the cities. Career education, with its immediate practicality and extended options, offers the best chance to make a secondary education more responsive to the economic and social needs of minorities.

Educators must come to terms with the fact that sooner or later every student must work. What is needed is an understanding that "future carpenters" are as important as "future teachers"—and that the school must not foreclose from the future teacher the very useful option of becoming a carpenter.

Career education within the schools can build on established curricula. Vocational education, despite its faults, is by far the most advanced and sophisticated of existing career education programs. The first step forward should be refinement and expansion of existing vocational programs.

The essential component of the Commission's proposal is the proliferation of work-study programs. Instead of functioning in isolation from the community, the school must literally extend itself into the community and utilize all the community's offerings for work and service. The goal is for students to have access to training in any occupation carried on in the community served by the school. This approach avoids the expenditure of vast amounts of money for the expansion of vocational shops, and it obviously improves to a large degree the realism of the instruction.

Career contracting should become an integral part of the curricula of secondary schools. Care must be taken that the job site does not become as custodial as the school has been. Signing the contract, the businessman must undertake to develop specific competencies in students in return for his fee.

In addition to expanding the general offerings in vocational education at minimal cost, contracting offers a means of providing training for a great variety of interests. A school may have, for example, a few students interested in watchmaking. There would not be enough of them to justify a course in a vocational shop. Under a contracting arrangement, however, the limit on the program would be the number of watchmakers in the community (which reflects economic reality) rather than the number of students who wish to sign up. The per pupil cost for training under contract is much lower than the cost of training in a vocational shop located at the school.

Another major priority is the establishment of area vocational training programs or schools designed to teach hard skills. Such schools should serve younger students preparing for apprenticeships, and should not attempt to supplant existing businesses as training agencies. In general, vocational schools should not duplicate community facilities such as automobile mechanic shops. Such elaborate facilities should be brought under the rubric of secondary education and become an integral part of the school's contracted program.

A truly broad and comprehensive vocational program must also accommodate adults and adolescents who leave school with insufficient occupational skills. Both groups require recycling opportunities. The objective should be easy exit from school and entry into work-related study programs.

Obviously, school personnel alone cannot carry out this proposal. Large-scale community participation will be required, and the participation must be felt at the administrative and planning levels as well as on the job. Meanwhile, the school must overcome the inflexibility of curricula which rigidly separates academic and vocational programs.

Occupational Proficiency

An important component of the Commission's proposal for career education is that a massive effort be made to assist all secondary students in attaining occupational effectiveness. The Commission is aware that this objective does not define itself. The issue was put into focus by the American Vocational Association:

> Each set of educational aims formulated during the past century has included preparation for occupational proficiency as one of its major aims. But what constitutes preparation for occupational proficiency? There is no major agreement on this point. Some would hold that the development of basic educational skills and work habits would constitute preparation for occupational proficiency. Others hold that preparation includes skill, knowledge, habit, and attitude development leading to salable competencies in the labor market.[6]

The Commission takes the position that the acquisition of basic educational skills and work habits is a necessary part of preparation for occupational proficiency. The first purpose of the school is to equip the student with the tools of learning. This objective may not be tampered with.

Proposal for Career Education

The Commission's career education proposal is divided into three phases. Phase one is a program in career awareness. Its objectives are to develop in all students an overview of various careers, respect for the work ethic, and an appreciation of the dignity of work. Its foundation is an understanding that all honest work and purposeful study are respectable, that the kingdom can still be lost for want of a nail. Teachers involved in the program must continually broaden their knowledge of different careers.

The second phase of the career education program is designed for students in grades 8 through 10. Exploratory opportunities are provided through a variety of "career clusters." Some fifteen such clusters, covering approximately 800 occupations, have already been developed by the U.S. Department of Labor. Students who investigate several occupations in each of a number of clusters will develop skills and acquire information important to them in making the choices they will have to make.

In a school district which has several secondary schools, located reasonably near each other, different clusters can be presented in different schools, with transportation for students whose primary interest is in a cluster not offered at their home school. Such arrangements assure diversity of programs at acceptable cost.

Phase three of career education includes extensive opportunities for students in grades 11 and 12 to concentrate on the acquisition of specific skills related to the occupations they have chosen. Career counselors must be certain that these occupations are in demand, important to society, and fulfilling for the individuals who choose them.

The Job Market and Placement

Statistics developed by the U.S. Department of Labor argue that "eight out of ten jobs to be filled during the 1970s will be open to people who have not completed four years of college."[7]

This projection is further supported by the 1972–73 edition of the *Occupational Outlook Handbook*, the government's encyclopedia of employment information designed to help young people choose careers.

Such jobs include as a tiny sample: business machine servicemen, construction machinery operators, stewardesses, hospital attendants, receptionists, electronic computer operators, and cashiers. Although many jobs can be learned after employment, requirements for entry to training will continue to rise during the 1970s, and young people who receive vocational orientation in high school will be better equipped to compete for these openings. As industrial processes, technology, and business procedures increase in complexity, more jobs will require more training.

Since job placement is essential to the success of career education programs, publications such as the *Occupational Outlook Handbook* must be continuously available to students and counselors. Careful and accurate analyses of the local job market must be made. No career education program can be considered successful unless it leads to employment in a satisfying occupation. The chance of achieving this result will be much greater if the schools work in close collaboration with the state employment services.

Counseling and Job Placement

In many schools, counselors are a hindrance, not a help, to adolescents who would benefit from career programs. Traditionally, school counselors are teachers with three or more years of teaching experience who have taken college courses in the area of counseling and guidance. The counselor's job is often considered a way station on the road to an administrative job. Not enough counselors are knowledgeable about the job market, or about the world at work. This is nonsense, it must be recognized as such, and it must stop. Experience at an employment office is probably better background for a high school counselor than experience in a classroom. Many counselors should have both backgrounds.

Counselors should also have enough sympathy for the students and understanding of on-the-job conditions to be supportive rather than critical when students request transfers from one training situation to another or from one career opportunity to another. The school must be sufficiently flexible in its program to permit students to change their choices.

The payoff from the work of the counselor's office is measurable and should be measured: success on the school-related job, placement in a real job for those who want it.

Granting Credit for Work Experiences

Because the primary purpose of career education programs in secondary schools is to provide marketable skills for students, credit toward completion of the requirements for graduation should be granted for skills developed outside the school program.

Many students work at afternoon, weekend, and summer jobs that amount to "on-the-job-training" in a variety of occupations. Credit should be given for these experiences, based on knowledge attained and competence demonstrated in skills related to the job.

Granting credit for work experience can be a way to persuade adolescents who have dropped out of school that they should return and finish whatever remains to be done to qualify for a diploma. Every high school should establish procedures for crediting nonschool work experience. The proclaimed "alternative school" is not the only school that needs alternative paths to the secondary credential.

The Commission notes with satisfaction the recent relaxation of some of the federal and state constraints which have tended to polarize the vocational curricula. Additional relaxation of constraints must be made wherever they prohibit local authorities from offering curricula with the fullest possible options and choices.

NOTES

1. National Advisory Council on Vocational Education, *Vocational Education Amendments of 1968*, P.L. 90–576, Annual Report (Washington, D.C.: Department of Health, Education, and Welfare, July 15, 1969).

2. Dr. Nolan Estes, general superintendent of the Dallas, Texas, school district in a report to the Commission on Mar. 5, 1973.

3. Department of Health, Education, and Welfare, Publication No. (OE) 72-39.

4. Frank Newman et al., *Report on Higher Education* (Washington, D.C.: Government Printing Office, March 1971), p. 2.

5. Remarks to the Commission by Roman C. Pucinski at Dallas, Texas, Mar. 6, 1973.

6. Report of AVA Task Force on Career Education, American Vocational Association, Washington, D.C., n.d., p. 26.

7. "Job Prospects in the 1970s Outlined in New Guide," U.S. Department of Labor News Release, USDL-72-148, Apr. 3, 1972, p. 1.

CHAPTER 6

Global Education
as Part of the Curriculum

Recommendation No. 11: Global Education

The education of the nation's adolescents must be superior to that of their parents. Part of this superiority must be an enhanced sense of the globe as the human environment, and instruction to this end must reflect not only the ancient characteristics of the world, but emerging knowledge of biological and social unity. All secondary school students should receive a basic global education.

New instructional material for global education must be prepared if this recommendation is to be effective. State departments of education should require teacher training institutions to design programs which prepare teachers to present such programs.

The components of secondary school curricula which relate to international affairs have traditionally appealed only to high-ability, college-bound students. The world is now too small for that. Not only the great matters of war and peace, but small decisions made far away will affect the everyday lives of ordinary people in America. They should learn about them.

For ten years fighting in Indochina and the threat of the draft kept the issue of war and peace front and center for the average adolescent. Though the draft is over and America's war has stopped, the issues are no less vital. Television gives students daily reports of international events, but often in a way that conceals the implications. The school has a central role to play.

The second force bringing global consideration to the forefront is the growing interdependency of nations. A recent investigation of America's international economic involvements concluded: "By the end of the century, it now appears that the United States will be dependent on foreign supplies not only for the major share of its petroleum but also for the major share of 12 of the 13 basic industrial raw materials required by a modern industrial economy."[1]

The world is rapidly becoming an integrated system geographically, economically, and technologically. An inventory of the connections that make up interdependency must include (1) instantaneous communication and fast travel worldwide, (2) a complex international monetary system, (3) the operation of multinational corporations and the international trade-union movement growing in response, (4) domestic ecological consequences of actions by other nations, some very distant from our shores, and (5) overall limitations of natural resources.

In spite of a rapidly developing interdependence among nations and the universal urge for a new commitment to world peace, very little is being done in the United States to educate young people to cope with significant global issues. Few students from inner-city schools or school districts with low-income families are given even an introduction to these subjects. Research makes it clear that international education as

now taught in the nation's high schools is an elitist subject. In
the future, America's high schools must present global studies
as a concern of all students.

Toward a Definition

When a change in curriculum is prescribed for all students,
definitions are needed. The term "international education" is
not usually distinguished from such related terms as "world
affairs" and "global studies." In these pages, the term "global
education" is used to refer to a broader interaction than is
implied by the terms "international" or "intergovernmental."
Global education, in the perspective of a curriculum for both
college preparatory and non-college-bound students, is concerned with scientific, ecological, and economic issues which
affect everyone. These include questions of war and peace,
interdependency of natural resources, climate control, the use
of the sea bed, the population issue, and other concerns where
national positions are not necessarily controlled by inherited,
prescientific, political positions.

In contrast, the phrase "international education" is used to
denote issues reflecting a relationship or conflict of interest
between nations. Starting with global and going down to national, the issues as traditionally presented seem to become
more controversial.

Though secondary educators have been struggling with
international education for college-bound students for a number of years and many organizations and foundations are engaged in supporting international education, there has never
been any agreement or clear statement as to the objectives of
programs in international studies. Unrelated courses in geog-
raphy, world history, and foreign languages are usually regarded as adequate to meet the need, with area studies as an
option in innovative suburban schools. There is no movement
in the United States today to expand international studies

beyond what is now provided in the eleventh and twelfth grades to students who are college-bound. The Commission hopes to provoke such a movement.

Basic International Literacy

What must be sought is basic international literacy. This was in years past a target of social studies instruction in the elementary school, which proceeded by "widening circles," from the family in the early years to a worldwide focus in the sixth grade. What must be learned is now too important and too involved to be confined to instruction in the elementary school, and the incidental international learnings from work in the foreign language and social studies departments have proved insufficient.

In such a course a student would be expected to acquire, among other things, a sense of the climate and natural resources of different parts of the world, and the economic production and trade routes that result. The course should include (1) enough history and politics to demonstrate that viewpoint evolves from heritage, that things look different according to where the looker is; (2) enough economics to make apparent the doctrine of comparative advantage; and (3) enough anthropology to permit an informed, private view of the extent to which men are alike and different according to their cultures.

Beyond these academic requirements, global studies must be seen as a science of survival. Benjamin Franklin's observation of the interdependence of the American revolutionists—that if they did not hang together they would all hang separately—now applies worldwide. Most important of all, the interdependence of peoples in the modern world means that intelligent, political participation requires understanding that transcends the ethnocentricity of today's conventional high school program.

Basic international literacy involves an understanding of

five interrelated concepts: (1) the fact of cultural pluralism, (2) the nature of international violence, (3) the culture and standard of living of various people, (4) the practice of social justice among the communities of the world society, and (5) the interdependency of survival.

The ability to manage these concepts has value for virtually everyone. Those members of the affluent sectors of American society will have many reasons to use this knowledge in their individual vocations and vacations. In addition, ever increasing numbers of working-class Americans find that the big jet and the packaged tour have brought foreign travel within their means. As the trade unions of the world begin to coordinate their struggles with multinational corporations, factory workers will find that decisions of great immediate importance to them, in which they personally participate, have an international component.

Decline in Foreign Language Study

Another factor compelling global studies in the secondary schools is the sharply declining enrollment in foreign languages. Many students have found in a foreign language a way to escape the narrow vision of an upbringing in the confines of a single culture, but shrinking enrollments in foreign languages make their impact questionable. Partly because all their students do take foreign languages—usually English— the schools of other countries now offer what most observers regard as an education in global affairs superior to that in America. Because they study English in a practical, contemporary way, adolescents in other countries tend to know what is happening in the United States; but adolescent Americans know little of what is happening abroad. Recently, the European Economic Community (commonly known as the Common Market), which has great impact on American employment and the American standard of living, commissioned a study of American attitudes toward European economic unity. The first finding in the study, performed by Gallup International, was that 55 percent of Americans had never heard of the Common Market.

The New York Times, through its responsibilities as an international newspaper, has probably been more concerned about the foreign language problem than any other publication directed to a general audience. Over the last three years, the *Times* has made numerous surveys of the teaching of foreign languages and has viewed the findings with alarm. Fred M. Hechinger of the *Times* editorial board recently wrote about this issue:

> Foreign languages have never been classroom favorites. Students took them as they would cod liver oil—and could do little about it. But today, as part of the general youth revolution, requirements have eased and language study is a casualty.
>
> . . . What are the reasons for the present trend? Aside from the student rebellion with its attack on required courses, some observers believe there has been a general turning away from "hard" subjects in favor of involvement with social issues which were considered by many of the rebels as more relevant. . . . [2]

Language studies may also be suffering the consequences of a widely accepted innovation that failed. Decline of interest in language has accompanied the spread of the language laboratory. Most studies show the language laboratory as no more efficient than traditional classrooms in teaching foreign languages. Meanwhile, laboratory procedures may have over-emphasized the skills side of the subject at the expense of all that makes foreign language learning an enjoyable and challenging experience.

The good foreign language teacher interacting with a class, employing the traditional methods for teaching foreign languages creates a social climate of excitement in the classroom;

by contrast, most students find the language laboratory dull. It is highly questionable whether the technology of the laboratory is an improvement over the social system created by the use of the chalkboard, utilizing face-to-face interactions of student and teacher and of students with each other.

Of course, others have more incentive to learn English than Americans have to study foreign languages. English is the language of the multinational corporations, nurtured originally in the American capital market, and of international air travel. Approaching Moscow airport, a Swedish jet pilot will speak to the ground controllers in English. The establishment of United Nations Headquarters in New York meant that the language of diplomacy, which for three hundred years had been French, would become English. The factors that created this dependence on America are now gone, but neither students nor teachers know it; there is a widespread belief in America that for all practical purposes, English is enough.

Travel—especially a chance to spend some time *living* in a foreign country—is one of the few things that really convince large numbers of students that a foreign language is important. Even when this opportunity is offered, poor preparation and the inferior quality of the exchange programs diminish its value. Nevertheless, increased exchange programs for both students and teachers would seem the most direct route to major reform in foreign language teaching. Not all the omens are unfavorable. Many foreign language teachers in the United States are now beginning to change the focus of their instruction. Because of the almost universal abandonment of the language requirement for college admission, the captive audience is no longer there. The need to recruit a voluntary audience and to reduce the elitist components in the instructional methods (such as travel abroad) has encouraged many foreign language teachers to think about the needs of a larger share of the secondary population, including students of all abilities and backgrounds.

Nevertheless, on balance, the existing foreign language curriculum is in trouble in the nation's high schools, colleges, and universities. A growing number of colleges and universities, including Yale, Stanford, Brown, Trinity, and Wesleyan have abolished the language requirement not only for entrance but for graduation. The elimination of requirements also eliminates much of the incentive for studying a foreign language in high school. Indeed, Ohio State University no longer requires a proficiency in foreign languages for some of its Ph.D.s.

The collapse of foreign language teaching strengthens the case for a systematic program of global education. Unfortunately, this means yet another subject in an already crowded curriculum. Several disciplines encompass aspects of the study of global affairs, but in the final analysis the requirement must be that international education pervade the entire curriculum, beginning in grade 1.

American history is, of course, the subject most amenable to modification for this purpose. In most states American history is offered at least three times—usually in the fifth, eighth, and eleventh grades. All three courses should include work on the changing relations of the United States and the rest of the world. The third course should be heavily weighted with material on international understanding and misunderstanding, and on the fundamental interdependence of the nations of the modern world.

Another course easily changed is "Problems of Democracy." Most often this course deals with current events, the drug problem, prejudice and discrimination, bigness in American life, the democratic system, urbanization, and a variety of other social issues. Courses under this title might well be oriented toward the impact of the world on the United States and it on the world. As the specialized social sciences and ecological sciences are introduced in the secondary curriculum, attention should be paid to the opportunities they offer for establishing a global perspective.

The suggested retrenchment in the teaching of American history should not be interpreted as downgrading the school's role in acculturating adolescents. Comparative studies cannot and should not be value-free. Loyalties to nations, loyalties to ethnic groups, loyalties to localities, and to families are important to the mental health of the student and the social health of the community and should remain central in the educational process. There should be no conflict between these loyalties properly interpreted and a sense of belonging to the family of man and the growing world community.

Though the need is obvious as soon as it is mentioned, global studies will not automatically enter the secondary curriculum. Someone will have to decide on objectives, and define in measurable terms what it is that all students should understand in order to function intelligently in the twenty-first century. Teachers should be prepared to provide the necessary information in a variety of delivery systems, for example, history, economics, social science, and foreign language.

The nation's teacher preparation programs should speak very clearly to global education. New materials will be needed for use in existing course structures and to serve as foundation stones for the new courses that must be created. The Commission calls on the educational leadership to assure that tomorrow's students will grasp the global issues that relate to the security and well-being of the United States.

NOTES

1. Lester R. Brown, *The Interdependence of Nations,* Overseas Development Council, Development Paper 10, 1972, p. 7.
2. Fred M. Hechinger, "Language Study: Alarm at the Decline," *The New York Times,* Aug. 27, 1972.

PART IV

ALTERNATIVES TO TRADITIONAL SECONDARY EDUCATION

CHAPTER 7

Nonformal Sources of Secondary Education

Recommendation No. 12: Alternative Paths to High School Completion

A wide variety of paths leading to completion of requirements for graduation from high school should be made available to all students. Individual students must be encouraged to assume major responsibility for the determination of their educational goals, the development of the learning activities needed to achieve those goals, and the appraisal of their progress.

Recommendation No. 13: Local Board Responsibilities for Funding Alternatives

Whenever a student chooses an acceptable alternative to the comprehensive high school, local school boards should fund his education at the level of current expenditure computed for other students.

Recommendation No. 14: Credit for Experience

Secondary schools should establish extensive programs to award academic credit for accomplishment outside the build-

*ing, and for learning that occurs on the job, whether the job
be undertaken for pay, for love, or for its own sake. Community involvement will, of course, be required in such a
program and should be as encompassing as possible.*

**Recommendation No. 15: Secondary Level Examination Pro-
gram**

*The College Level Examination Board should expand its
College Level Examination Program to include a comparable
Secondary Level Examination Program. The tests should be
routinely administered quarterly or monthly to help adolescents to obtain credit for work done outside the classroom.*

The sources of educational experiences are relatively unimportant; what matters is whether or not they deliver the
knowledge and skills required by the learners. It should make
no difference whether these are acquired through formal
courses within school buildings or through action-learning
programs. The degree to which goals are achieved, not the
manner of instruction, should be the basis on which the effectiveness of a school is assessed.

James Coleman summed up youths' need for an avenue
other than formal schooling for growing up—another way of
transition from adolescence to adulthood—in the following
manner:

. . . Previously, it was natural that schooling could have
been confused with education—for schooling was that
part of the education of the young which took place for-
mally, and thus had to be planned for and consciously
provided. But the larger part of education took place
outside the school. The child spent most of his time outside the school; school was a small portion of his existence. It taught him to read and write and work with
numbers, but the most important parts of education it
did not provide: learning about work, both the skills and
the habits, learning how to function in society, learning

how to be a father or mother, husband or wife, learning to take care of others and to take responsibility for others. Because these things were learned informally, through experience, or at least without formal organization, they could be disregarded, and "education" could come to be identified with "schooling."

. . . Thus although schooling remains a small portion of education, it occupies an increasingly larger portion of a young person's time, while the remaining portion of his education is *not* well provided by ordinary, everyday, unplanned activities. Consequently, if an appropriate reform of education is to be made, it must begin with this fact: schooling is not all of education, and the other parts of education require just as much explicit planning and organization as does schooling.[1]

The Commission urges secondary school educators to recognize that authentic learning can take place in a wide variety of settings, many of them remote from the schoolhouse. Learnings derived from out-of-school sources can contribute effectively to both the intellectual and affective growth of young people. Therefore, credit should be awarded for nontraditional and nonformal learning experiences which produce meaningful progress toward the established goals of secondary education.

Many schools are already reaching out to use the broader community in the education of their students. It is no longer unusual for schools to offer programs in cooperative work-study, service projects, educational travel, cross-age tutoring, and a host of similar nonclassroom experiences. The Commission endorses these forms of direct learning and encourages their expansion. These are nontraditional paths to learning, alternatives to the conventional classroom program, still under the direct and immediate control of the school. They extend the classroom into the world beyond, but they remain part of an education patterned by the school.

By the end of the seventies, the Commission expects that all schools will also grant credit for nonformal modes of learning whenever they are of proven educational value. Non-formal learning experiences are those that fall outside the confines of the school. They are the education indirectly, even unknowingly, derived from each individual's many encounters with his world. They are the things he may learn as hobbies or special interests, things he learns in the work-place, his social and personal transactions with his surroundings. They are the books he reads just because he wants to read them, the music he hears, the television to which he is exposed.

Philosophical difficulties arise in any attempt to equate a secondary education with a high school diploma. If secondary education comprises an age-appropriate intellectual, emotional, and value growth *process*, as many thoughtful educators believe, then the observable, measurable outcomes may be rather low-order indicators of the value of what has happened. It is easier to determine the specific knowledge or skills young people should have upon the completion of secondary school than to discern the subtle changes which validate the meaning of secondary education.

Indeed, when one talks of granting "credit" for life and growth activities that occur beyond the purview of the school, the reference is really not to education, but to credentials. As long as education continues to serve as a societal sorting-out process, however, the credentials themselves will have an existence and a significance quite separate from the educational process. If the high school diploma is to be a threshold to the future for young people—and not a formidable, perhaps impossible barrier for not an inconsiderable number of them—steps must be taken to make the awarding of the certificate consonant with all experiences that make up a truly secondary education. The schools must learn to recognize in conventional ways the unconventional but valid education of their students.

The Commission, of course, does not argue that all non-formal learning experiences merit high school credit. Secondary education does imply the acquisition of a fairly well defined body of knowledge and skills, although these can be attained at varying levels of intensity. Informally acquired learnings must relate to the goals of secondary education if credit is to be granted toward high school completion. Whenever a student can demonstrate that he commands the competencies being sought in any specific high school course, he should be granted credit. The fact that he did not "take" the course is irrelevant.

Unfortunately, specific instructional objectives have been determined for very few high school subjects. This makes it hard to equate the competencies acquired by the student in out-of-school circumstances with those he would have been expected to attain in a course. Many educators would argue, however, that a professionally trained teacher's interpretation of the results of a course are more valid than measurements of narrow behavioral objectives. What is needed is professional judgment.

Nonformal Sources of Learning

A stimulating, multidimensioned culture is in itself educative. Few educators would argue that their ardent critics are entirely wrong in their claim that by shutting off the young person from the swirling, living currents of his culture, schools stultify rather than foster his growth and development. Much genuine learning obviously takes place outside the formal structure of organized education. Schools must learn to take fuller advantage of all the learning opportunities young people enjoy, and where these opportunities cost money the school boards should be prepared to spend it, up to a limit set by the average current expenditure computed for students in the formal program. Public policy should allow the money to follow the student.

Because students spend so much time listening and viewing, commercial and educational radio and television offer possibilities for functional education. Students need not be in school to write themes and compositions, compose short stories and music, produce plays, and learn about law enforcement, court procedures, and citizens' rights under the Constitution. Enterprising teachers who capitalize on the offerings of the media can raise the achievement levels of students. High school credit must be granted for significant gains in understanding and knowledge as the result of radio and television exposure.

An attempt to structure nonformal education (which is almost but not quite a contradiction in terms) is the newspaper project being developed by the extension division of the University of California at San Diego. This is an effort to make college-level courses available through the daily newspaper. These newspaper courses are now being designed to serve three audiences: the casual reader whose interest might be caught by the information presented; the more serious reader who wants to explore a subject; and the reader seeking college credit for a course as part of his program of studies.

Similar programs must be developed at the secondary level, both for adults seeking to complete their high school diploma work and for young people currently enrolled in regular schools. Newspapers clearly have advantages over radio and television: the newspaper comes into the home in permanent form, can be read at the student's convenience, and can be kept for subsequent referral and rereading.

Public libraries also offer great potential for helping people continue with high school work outside the school. Libraries have already begun to serve as coordinating, learning, extension, and testing centers for people seeking to complete their secondary education. Librarians need help from other educators to fulfill these functions, and the libraries need funds to remain open (as nearly all of them did years ago) at night and on Sundays and holidays.

Action-Learning

Action-learning programs must be accepted as a source of learning experiences. These programs, initiated and supervised by schools, involve student volunteers in the activities of social service agencies. Students are under the immediate direction of persons who work for agencies other than the school.

Action-learning places students in direct contact with social problems and offers them opportunities to assist in their resolution. What is learned is immediately reinforced because the learner sees evidence of the effects of his individual actions.

ORGANIZING AND IMPLEMENTING ACTION-LEARNING PROGRAMS

The scope of an action-learning program should be limited only by the availability of service agencies within the community. Some schools have almost unlimited possibilities for student involvement; others may have only a few. Almost every school in the nation will have access to eight basic types of agencies: senior citizens' organizations, ecological groups, hospital service units, voter registration groups, mental health offices, school tutorial services, child day-care centers, and government bureaus.

The school bears major responsibility for organizing, implementing, and evaluating an action-learning program. Staffing needs include a program coordinator and leaders for seminars at which student volunteers can compare notes and find out what they are supposed to learn next. The seminars must be planned to link the academic program and the action-learning program.

The school, the agency, and the student should cooperatively evaluate student progress. Student participation in evaluation is essential to the program. The student who has set his own goals and then measures his own progress toward them becomes by definition self-directed.

Students should decide for themselves, with counseling, how much time they wish to spend in the program. Participation may range from a few hours per week to half of each school day. In some instances, students who have already met the minimum academic requirements for graduation will choose to enter full-time service, earning elective credits to complete their high school career.

Alternative Routes to the High School Credential

Outside the school system, Americans young and old are already educating themselves at employer-based learning centers, predischarge programs in the military services, home-study programs (though the completion rate here is distressingly low), and the various street academies. The Commission believes that many of these outside establishments provide valid learning experiences for young people and should be recognized as participants in the process of secondary education. If a student can present evidence of growth and achievement related to these outside programs, the school should grant credit for the work done.

There are, of course, problems of motivation when a student is working without the immediate support of a sympathetic adult and his peers in the school community. Obviously, some experiences are educationally much more valuable than others. Conscientious schoolmen will find it hard to establish criteria controlling the credit given for nonformal learning encounters. Both the students and the schools need the stimulus of variety.

In other countries, the secondary leaving certificate is awarded on successful completion of an external examination: in theory, a French adolescent can receive a baccalaureate without ever going to school at all. In America, a high school diploma is usually based upon the acquisition of 16 or so discrete units of credit granted by a school. The thought is that the successful completion of a certain number of courses assures that a student has carried out the adolescent developmental tasks necessary for secondary education. That this premise has proven to be false in many cases does not completely invalidate the underlying approach. Certainly, exit testing presents grave problems of its own.

As long as the student remains in the mainstream of the high school and slowly—perhaps even painfully—accumulates his credits, the American system functions, more or less. The student earns his credits one by one, eventually reaching the required total, and receives a diploma.

Should the student sever himself from the system prior to graduation his chances of getting that diploma will greatly diminish. If he later decides he needs it, his options are limited. He may either resume the amassing of credits in a high school setting or take the General Educational Development tests, which certify the "equivalency" of a high school education.

Each route has strait gates. The student who returns to school must still earn his credits on the basis of time spent in class. If he dropped out early in the high school process, he may be confronted with a dreary vista of years to be traversed before he can take home a diploma. What he has learned in work and life goes unrecognized by the school. Few American educators have thought through the meaning of secondary education for adults.

Until recently, the GED "equivalency certificate" suffered from limited acceptance, but its utility today is almost comparable to that of a standard diploma. Many educators, however, continue to doubt its true "equivalency." The certificate is granted for accomplishment on a nonreferenced test, which measures each candidate's answers to a set of objective questions against a standard which is nothing more nor less than the proportion of similar questions correctly answered by the average high school graduate. The sample of knowledge and skills covered by the GED is much smaller and narrower than the abilities and attitudes developed in a valid secondary education.

Moreover, scores on the GED test can be raised by coaching. This would be acceptable on a criterion-referenced test like that of the National Assessment project, where the candidate's performance is compared not against the performance of other candidates but against a predetermined minimum acceptable accomplishment. Until a criterion-referenced GED test is developed, the fairness and usefulness of the equivalency certificate will remain in doubt.

The Commission urges both secondary school educators and test-makers to undertake an easier task: the construction of equivalency examinations not for secondary education as a whole but for the individual courses in the normal high school curriculum. These tests should be based on the stated objectives of the courses. Their content should assure that the successful candidate has an adequate command of the subject. His reward should be credit for the course, whether he has taken it or not.

This is not an impossible dream. The College Level Examination Program (CLEP), introduced in 1965 by the College Entrance Examination Board, has demonstrated the practicality of this procedure in higher education. Growing numbers of secondary school students are now receiving credit for college courses before attending their first college class. Some earn an entire year's credit through CLEP examinations before entering college.

The Commission recommends that CLEP be amplified into SLEP (School Level Examination Program), to permit students to demonstrate competence in high school as well as college courses.

State governments should assume the costs of both SLEP and CLEP examinations. The present fee of $15 per CLEP examination is prohibitive to many students, and the states save many times the cost of the examination when a student tests out of a year. The annual cost to state taxpayers for an undergraduate in a state school now averages more than $2,000. These benefits can also flow downward, as when students enter a college or community college after eleventh grade. Obviously, any institution that gives high school credits for work done out of school would have to accept college credits as fulfillment of graduation requirements.

Any proposal that accelerates a student's rate of progress will be strongly resisted by those who lose the funds that would accrue. Many high schools will not grant a diploma to a student who takes his twelfth year at a college. Several state university faculty committees have attempted to ban the acceptance of CLEP credits. However, the academic community as a whole has confidence in the tests: CLEP results are being used as a basis for granting credit by 900 colleges in all states.

The Commission would not wish to see a European system imposed on American secondary education. External tests must never become the sole criterion for the high school diploma. Their value is as an alternative. In this focus, external tests may well be a necessity: without them, recognition of nonformal education will be severely limited. Alternative routes to a secondary education must be found so that adolescents can seek their goals through work experience, the marketplace, and the bustling crowds of humanity as well as through the school.

NOTE

1. "How Do the Young Become Adults?," paper presented by James S. Coleman at the American Educational Research Association Annual Meeting, Apr. 4, 1972, Chicago.

CHAPTER 8

The Impact of Television on Curriculum Content

Recommendation No. 16: Broadcast Television

Major funding sources, including both foundations and the National Institute of Education, should initiate and support extensive research into the influence of television on students' attitudes, perceptions, and life styles. The purpose of this research should be to suggest changes in school curricula and instructional approach.

The broadcasting industry should establish media fellowships designed to afford secondary school teachers and instructional leaders the opportunity to study the use of broadcast commercial television for educational purposes.

Recommendation No. 17: Classroom Use of Broadcast Material

Copyright laws and union contracts should be written to make sure that classroom use of broadcast materials copied off the air is not unnecessarily restricted. Television programs should never be asked to carry instructional burdens alone.

*Books and pamphlets must be specially and carefully prepared
to accompany all instruction via television. Both the instructional television program and the printed materials should be
available in public libraries as well as in schools.*

Recommendation No. 18: Cable Television

*When cable franchises are awarded, the local school system
should have exclusive use of three channels during the daytime, with possible use of more as needed. At least one—and
preferably all three—of these cable channels should continue
to be available for nighttime viewing by school students or
for purposes of adult education.*

Explanation of Terms

Following the guidance of the Carnegie report on public television,[1] the words "educational television" have been avoided
in these pages. The words "broadcast television" have been
used both for the profit-seeking efforts of commercial channels
and the entertainment and public-affairs programs of noncommercial "public television."

Material designed for specific educational use is called "instructional television." Such material may be broadcast on
commercial stations as a public service ("Sunrise Semester"),
or may be offered on noncommercial stations controlled by
citizen groups, schools, universities, or governments. "Instructional television" may also be presented on cable systems or
over closed-circuit systems within schools.

Broadcast Television

Practically every child in the United States has access to television. The 1970 census reported that 96 percent of all American homes contain at least one television set; more than one-
half have two or more. By the time an adolescent reaches high

school, he has spent as much time in front of a television set as he has in school. This fact alone would make today's student a different creature from the student of fifty years ago. What have the schools done to take advantage of this universal acquaintance with—indeed, addiction to—television? To what extent has television as a medium changed students' attitudes, perceptions, and life styles? Educators need answers to these and other significant questions before they can plan the secondary school of the future.

How much time do children spend watching television? The question is hard to answer because of the variation in viewing time from day to day by the same individual, and because of sex differences in program preferences, which surprisingly appear even before a child begins his schooling. Most children watch television at least two hours every day. Many spend much more time before the set. As many as a quarter of the students in the sixth grade, and almost the same fraction of tenth graders, watch at least five and one-half hours of television on any given school day.

Viewing reaches a peak toward the end of puberty, then starts to decline. Sixth graders spend more time before the set than either first graders or tenth graders. At the sixth-grade level, the heaviest viewers of television are the brightest students; but by the tenth grade, the most able adolescents watch much less television than their peers of average ability.

A quarter of a century after the national proliferation of a pervasive communication technique involving nearly all the nation's families, little is known of its impact on adolescent education. While much speculative material has been written on the effects of television, very little well-documented research has been published; and what data exist relate to the social rather than the educational effects of viewing.

These studies, however, do suggest at least some side effects with implications for education: (1) television has increased homogeneity in language, customs, and dress; (2) it has generated a new tolerance for violence; (3) it influences the consumer learnings of adolescents, especially the younger adolescents, who are more inclined to talk with their parents about consumption. Commercials, which take 10 to 20 percent of the time on profit-seeking channels, are probably the most "educational" factors in television.

While the depth of the linguistic effect of television is unknown, substantial covert learning is certainly taking place. There can be no doubt that television influences verbal behavior. Within two weeks after the phrase "Here come de judge" was used on the comedy show "Laugh-In," it was part of school conversation everywhere; the phrase "very interesting" also became a byword among the nation's adolescents within just a few days after it drew laughs on the same program.

Research is needed to determine the impact of television viewing and listening on perception, linguistic development, communication, and school socialization. Brian Groombridge of the Independent Broadcasting Authority in Britain argues persuasively that television leads children to synthetic as opposed to analytic modes of learning. Vicarious experience, which cannot be tested in the normal trial-and-error system of the learning process, would seem to hulk much larger in the background of today's adolescents than in the background of their parents or teachers. Fantasy has always had a life of its own, but when knowledge is obtained from the tube the line between fantasy and reality may be more difficult to draw. These are profound and difficult questions, but one need not accept the speculations of the television researchers to agree with Samuel Gibbons of Children's Television Workshop that an education which clashes with the expectations children have derived from television is likely to be ineffective.

In any event, the schools cannot wait for research to provide certainty. In dealing with television as with most phenomena, educators must proceed on the basis of the best information they can get.

Instructional Television

One of the monumental failures of modern education is the medium of instructional television. Television was highly touted in the late fifties as a cure for ineffective traditional teaching, and schools rushed out and purchased literally hundreds of thousands of television sets. But the twin locksteps of high school scheduling and television programming made the result a disaster for the secondary schools that seriously tried to follow through. The broadcast instructional television facility, with only a single channel, cannot present any program more than once a day, and high schools are organized to have different classes in the same subject meet the same teacher at different times rather than different teachers at the same time. To use instructional broadcasts, high schools had to go to very large group instruction or ask teachers to prepare a greater number of different subject matters each day. What came out of the tube did not seem worth the trouble. Elementary schools are less structured, can modify timetables more easily, and, despite skeptical comments, have maintained a continuing interest in instructional programming.

The scheduling problem can now be solved easily by the video tape recorder, but presently the schools are fundamentally disenchanted. At the outset, educators had assumed that television offered qualitative advantages in teaching over what was possible in the average traditional classroom. Proponents claimed that lessons could be more intelligently prepared and that charismatic teaching would be brought to all students everywhere. On the national scene, some of these hopes were realized: Berger Evans and Morton White became culture heroes. However, on the local level, which is where education happens, everyone has been disappointed.

Part of the difficulty here is the failure of broadcasters, researchers, and philosophers to answer fundamental questions about what the nature of television is. Everyone agrees that the live portrayal of events—from state funerals to moon walks to Super Bowls—is a glorious contribution from this astonishing technology. But most popular. American commercial television uses the medium merely as a way to distribute film. In instructional television, what has not been film has been lecture, most of it no better than a good, average live lecture by a local teacher, lacking all interaction between the teachers and the taught.

Questions have been raised as to the efficiency of televised instruction in standard-length presentation.

As one authority summed up the matter: "Television for most reasonably well-educated people is an extremely inefficient way to learn about anything. People really do learn at their own rate, and television is the most hopeless of lockstep classrooms, insisting that everyone in the audience work on the same time scale."[2]

Those engaged in the production of instructional television have wearied of their efforts to develop the schools as a market. James Koerner succinctly analyzed this situation.

In the 1960s the knowledge industry proceeded on the incredibly naive assumption that because education was a gigantic enterprise consuming $60 billion or $70 billion a year (it consumes more now) it constituted a massive market for educational technology. To their sorrow, the promoters learned that 70 percent and sometimes more of a typical school budget went to salaries, that another 15 to 20 percent was devoted to fixed costs, and that very little, if any, "loose" money was to be found in the average budget. They also failed to take into account the fact that professional politics, economic protectionism, and simple inertia are as alive and well in education as in any other large bureaucratic activity—meaning that big changes of any kind are rarely possible.[3]

Part of the problem with instructional television is that it has related too closely to the classroom. Its objectives have been excessively narrow, and its techniques have been too primitive. To accomplish its purposes, instructional television must become more like commercially oriented broadcast television in its technical quality and production values. Samuel Gibbons argues that richness of production values, by enabling quick children to find more in the picture than slow children find, gives a televised lesson some of the quality of individual instruction. At best, however, television cannot efficiently instruct by itself, and must become part of a system which relies also upon specially prepared printed materials and extensive teacher training.

Children's Television Workshop, producers of "Sesame Street" and "Electric Company," has much to teach the planners of television for secondary schools. So have the British, who have been at this business longer than Americans have, and more successfully. The British Broadcasting Corporation has concluded that programs designed for classrooms should last no longer than twenty minutes, leaving time for discussion. Not only teacher guides but printed materials for direct student use are prepared and distributed in advance to help create an ambience for useful discussion. The British Broadcasting Corporation and the Independent Broadcasting Authority (the British commercial broadcasting authority) invest considerable time and money in printed materials to go with instructional programs. Foundations and government agencies in America must do the same. As long as instructional television remains nothing more than viewing, it must remain a passive rather than an active element in secondary education.

The New Delivery Systems

In the late seventies, television will enter an era of abundance. Multichannel cables (linked by satellites) promise variety, flexibility, and an opportunity to use for educational purposes the simultaneity that is the glory of the broadcast media. Video casettes offer variety and flexibility of another kind, an audio-visual library teachers can command for individual purposes. Many schoolmen are not taking advantage of these possibilities. However, a few are making extensive use of video cassettes and closed circuit television.

The Video Cassette

The video cassette is already here, available for recording and playback of anything on the air or the cable, at prices that have begun to reach a realistic level for secondary schools. As volume increases, the hardware price will decrease even further, but video cassette players can be purchased now, even by schools with limited budgets. Many of these cassette players can be bought with relatively inexpensive camera units, allowing schools and classroom units to make their own materials for television. Unfortunately, the several different systems now available are incompatible with each other. Cassettes that play on one will not play on the others. Industry sources indicate that standardization is not expected before the late seventies.

Businesses are not waiting for standardization. Employment agencies are packaging interviews with job applicants and sending them out to prospective employers. These tapes give quick insight into an applicant's poise, knowledge, personality, and ability to communicate and handle himself. Ford Motor Company is using video cassettes to train salesmen for local dealers and to intrigue buyers. Other corporations are producing a wide variety of training programs for institutional use.

In school use the cassette tape can be stopped, repeated, or started at any point in the program. Some cassette systems would permit the teacher—or the school, or the system—to tailor-make inserts for splicing into the program. The cassette is far more versatile than 16mm film and shows promise of being substantially less expensive. The equipment is operable by the student. What he needs now is program material worth his attention—and positive attitudes from his teachers.

A question that must be answered soon, and may be answered wrong, is the extent to which broadcast programming, cultural and informational, commercial and noncommercial, can be copied off the air or the cable and then used for in-school instructional purposes. It reflects, in a large frame, the Xerox-copying problems now bemusing schools and universities, writers and publishers, Congress and the courts. The Commission lacks the expertise to make detailed recommendations in this highly technical area, and can only hope for a solution that will permit maximum use of the material without expropriating the legitimate interests of copyright holders, writers, and performers. Under foundation sponsorship, the television industry and the schools should try to work out ground rules of copyright and union contracts to make such material available in secondary education.

CABLE TELEVISION

Cable television is a delivery system for television programs, with the information traveling through high-capacity shielded wire rather than through the air. Because the signal, as it travels, does not escape the cable, the usual restriction on the number of channels that can be transmitted—the scarcity of spectrum space—does not exist.

The Federal Communications Commission has ordered every cable system with more than 3,000 subscribers to provide at least twenty channels and to reserve one for local schools as well as others for municipal government and public access. In some cities there may be an immense number of cable channels: a committee appointed to advise the city of Milwaukee has called for no fewer than 160 of them. These channels can be used to beam local programs into classrooms from local sources or (when the satellites fly) from a nationwide or worldwide cable network. It is by no means visionary to imagine a time when educational cable channels will offer live coverage of congressional hearings, appellate court arguments, medical operations, scientists' conventions—all at once. As cable franchises are awarded in cities around the country, school systems should insist that at least three channels be reserved for instructional use in the daytime. If new technology comes into being which creates more channels or allows for more sophisticated use, such as two-way communications, then the schools must be taken into consideration. Any change, either quantitative or qualitative, must include the schools.

Common sense would argue that television in the evening is the ideal medium for adult education, and Britain's Open University has demonstrated its utility for this purpose, though the television component is by no means the heart of the Open University program. In-school use of such material, however, is likely to be more effective. The effect of viewing a series of programs in an evening before the set is that each one is continuously being diluted by the program which follows it. A program seen in isolation has a greater chance to hold the attention and capture the memory.

Moreover, the new cable technology can be operated in an interactive mode. The FCC rules require all large cable systems to make technical provisions for feedback from the set to the originating "head end." Thus the straight-lecture syndrome, which has suffocated so much local effort in instructional television, can be alleviated by at least some unpredictable student responses from the classroom to the on-camera instructor.

Teacher Training

Among the differences between today's teachers and today's children is that the modes of perception of the children were affected from early childhood by television, which came into their teachers' lives only after basic learning patterns had been established. Teachers must become more involved in the shared environment of television. On an in-service basis, broadcasting companies, like textbook publishers, should send salesmen to the schools to introduce teachers to the planning behind the programs. (Such arrangements might be economically feasible as part of the copyright structure that will have to be built to legitimize and control copying by cassette recorders.) Meanwhile, the teacher training institutions must create pedagogic programs and courses to prepare new teachers, for whom television is now part of the natural landscape, not only in the use of in-school instructional television but also in the techniques of increasing the educational value of home viewing by their students.

Videotape can also be used to improve the quality and selection of teachers. Student teaching should be taped so that the young teacher himself, and those charged with his training, can observe and correct his performance. Self-observation, impossible otherwise, is especially important. In connection with their applications for teaching posts, teachers should be required to submit a videotaped lesson designed to give specific evidence of the applicant's teaching personality, ability to communicate with children in the classroom situation, voice projection, adeptness at interaction, and planning capabilities.

Broadcasters themselves should play a significant role in the schools' use of television. At the least, they can establish media fellowships to help teachers and instructional leaders bring new understanding of broadcasting to the educational community. There could be considerable public benefit from these ventures, for once secondary schools begin to use television purposefully, the tastes of the home audience might improve. Viewers who as students learned different ways of looking at television should be more sophisticated consumers of television—or at least one hopes so.

The Communications Act, under which broadcasters are licensed, requires them to serve educational as well as entertainment and commercial functions. The time has come for educators, broadcasters, and government to work out the ways in which the purpose of the Act can be achieved.

New Roles for Public Libraries

With the development of the video cassette recorder, the public library must anticipate a major change in function. It is destined to become the community bank for visual as well as printed media. The American Association of School Libraries has endorsed a national report recommending the unification of print and nonprint materials in media centers. With expansion of its previous print-oriented mission, the library will play a substantially increased role in education.

Meanwhile development of the university without walls, college credit by examination, and off-campus study programs will place enormous new demands on the library. As a free-access institution, the library must be the central resource for nontraditional approaches to education. When the library grasps this role, its educational function may come to equal or even surpass that of the traditional public schools. Alternative schools and programs at the secondary level will need the library at least as much as the nontraditional colleges will.

The Commission supports the efforts of the College Entrance Examination Board and its Library Independent Study Project, which seeks to convert the public library systems into a people's university. Ultimately, the project foresees a library including a learner's advisory service to help its customers not only with information and the choice of material but also with educational planning to assist the learner in his choice of goals. As the British Open University experience indicates, libraries should also expect to provide rooms and people for occasional group instruction and seminars.

NOTES

1. *Public Television: A Program for Action,* the Report and Recommendations of the Carnegie Commission on Educational Television (New York: McGraw-Hill, 1972).

2. Martin Mayer, *About Television* (New York: Harper & Row, 1972), p. 50.

3. James Koerner, "Educational Technology: Does It Have a Future in the Classroom?" *Saturday Review of Education,* May 1973, p. 44.

CHAPTER 9

Alternative Programs and Schools for Secondary Education

Recommendation No. 19: Flexibility of Alternative Programs

Differing time sequences—hourly, daily, weekly, yearly— must be made available so that educational programs can be adapted to the needs of individual students.

Schools are already moving away from the Carnegie Unit and beginning to grant credit on the basis of competence, demonstrated experience, and a host of other assessments. It is recommended that this practice be expanded and that the Carnegie Unit become merely one of the alternative ways of granting credit.

Recommendation No. 20: Rank in Class

Articulation between secondary schools and post-secondary schools must be improved, with each level seeking to support the educational efforts of the other. Personnel representing both levels must cooperatively develop alternatives to grade-

point average and rank in class for assessing the scope and quality of the education received by students at the secondary level. High schools should stop calcuating student rank in class for any purpose.

Many adolescents are poorly accommodated in today's conventional high schools. While dropout statistics are not reliable, census figures show that more than 40 percent of the population over the age of twenty-two does not possess a high school diploma. At least a million adolescents a year drop out of school. Few students announce that they are dropping out; most are embarrassed at leaving and give moving away as their reason for withdrawal. In reality, most of them are taking leave of school because they feel uncomfortable in the school's environment.

An equally pressing secondary school problem is the large group of students who have become disenchanted with the way things are but remain in school restlessly and reluctantly. Not all of this group are academically troubled. They are a mixed bag, sampling all levels of ability and social class background.

The cost to society is high. Continuation programs for dropouts alone involve so many different federal agencies that it is hard to estimate the cost. One recent report of research into the dropout matter counted thirty-three varieties of basic educational programs financed through eleven agencies of the federal government. The report described the many competing agencies as "a cacophony of splintered jurisdictions. . . ."[1] Dwarfing these figures, however, is the long-term social cost of the ineffectiveness of the schools, measured to the society in welfare, unemployment, and crime, and to the individual in loss of pride and a sense of personal failure.

The recent rise of alternative programs within conventional schools offers the public schools new hope that they can keep their promise of serving everyone. Such alternatives must entail more than mere freedom of educational choice in the matter of career goals and academic pursuits. The options must speak directly to the broad diversity of learning styles, living modes, cultural aspirations, value systems, and growth patterns that characterize adolescents. To impose a monolithic, unitary system of schooling upon young people is to deny and stultify individual and group differences which are the strength and promise of the nation.

The American educational community has only recently come to these beliefs. Accepting the need to establish free schooling as a right, the architects of the American system of education had centered on the common school as their major vehicle. During a period when the nation was seeking to hew out a single identity from widely divergent sources, uniformity of schooling seemed to offer the best approach. Fallacious as the "melting pot" concept may have been, it served for decades as the major impulse for the common schools.

During the 1960s the eruption of long-pent-up frustrations disclosed deep fissures in the nation. Educators began to heed the rising demand for a personal education, going beyond individualization of instruction to the provision of basically different means, perhaps even different ends, for the individual student. Fitting the school to the student, providing him with meaningful options for his own style of learning in the context of his own aspirations, became thinkable.

The Commission recognizes the historic and significant role the comprehensive high school has played in American education. However, it believes that the near-monopoly of secondary education by that institution, with its relatively standardized formats and restricted options, must now give way to a more diversified system of alternative schools and programs.

Secondary educators should carefully consider the concept of "alternativeness"—the development of a wide-ranging system of alternative programs to give a meaningful freedom of educational choice to every student. Every adolescent should, with proper guidance, be able to select those forms of schooling and learning most congenial to his basic learning style, philosophical orientation, and tastes.

The standard comprehensive high school, seeking to educate its diverse student body within the traditional context, undoubtedly will remain the keystone of the system of alternative schools. The Commission expects church-related schools to continue to play an important role in American secondary education. Indeed, as these schools clarify their own missions, they may be able to offer increasingly meaningful educational options to young adolescents. Independent schools, never comprehensive in the pattern of the public schools, may become a more important source of alternative programs and approaches. The proponents of "voucher" systems—which would permit parents to award to schools of their own choosing the tax money that would be spent on their child in public school —are, in essence, arguing for a way to finance independent alternative schools. Nonpublic schools, including independent and church-related institutions, must be included in any system of educational alternatives if effective freedom of choice is to be given all students.°

In the original plan proposed by the Commission, a study of nonpublic schools had been proposed; unfortunately it was not possible to undertake this study. Too often, the contributions of nonpublic schools to legitimate and needed pluralism in American education has been beclouded by the Constitutional limits on federal and state aid to nonpublic schools. This Commission fared no better than other groups, which have tried to consider the impact of nonpublic schools on American education, in avoiding the lack of resolution on the Constitutional issue.

In many ways, because these schools do operate without

° The Commissioners debated, extensively, the question of whether public funds should be made available for nonpublic alternative schools, but could reach no agreement.

benefit of public funds, they do provide leadership and opportunities which are denied to public education. These schools keep alive the concept that the private citizen has the right to seek for his child a type of schooling which best reflects the philosophy of life which he accepts and by which he lives. Freedom of educational choice is a precious heritage guaranteed by the Supreme Court in the case of *Pierce v. Sisters of Charity*, 1925.

Church-related schools firmly believe that value education is an integral part of schooling and gives meaning to education in a free society. Their focus on a value-oriented education is a significant reminder to educators in public schools that they too must focus on values even as they avoid the issues of establishment of religion or the indoctrination of students in value systems identified with specific religious sects.

The variety of alternative schools in American education will be limited only by the legitimate needs of adolescents and the vivacity of the imagination of educational planners. Mobile schools, street academies, action education, academic and vocational apprenticeships, and schools without walls will all be components of a system of alternatives in secondary schooling. Each will be designed to serve its own self-selected clientele. Finally, a sharply expanded program of continuing and adult secondary education will have to be made available to give young people time options as well as instructional choices. School must be not only "where you find it," but "when you want it."

Not the least of the practical difficulties of such a varied educational system will be the development of techniques to inform students of the variety and significance of choices available to them. Enrollment in any format—a classical college-preparatory school, a comprehensive high school, a career-based program, or a newly minted free school—must be completely voluntary. Students should not be pushed into alternatives. The student's personal characteristics and tastes must determine the school or the program in which he enrolls.

Though teaching and learning strategies will differ markedly from one school format to another, the fundamental goals of American education must remain constant. Every school within the system of alternatives must provide its students with the basic learning skills, social understanding, democratic orientations, personal values, and career clarifications that everyone needs. Moreover, the leaders of every school and every program must work to keep self-selection from becoming self-segregation. Care must be taken that irrelevant prerequisites do not screen out any aspiring student from any alternative program or school.

Alternative schools will have to be assessed rigorously against their stated purposes and the needs of their students. Any secondary school program, whether advertised as solidly conventional or as explosively experimental, must provide meaningful and coherent educational experience for its students. These experiences must contribute to the achievement of the goals of secondary education.

Alternatives should not be confused with the normal enrichment or elective educational experiences now offered in many schools. The intent of alternative schools and programs is to offer significant learning-style options to students, as well as to provide a milieu suited to the personal living and growing pattern of individuals. Each student should be able to match his cognitive and affective responses with a school setting especially appropriate for him.

Certainly, some of the emerging practices in both conventional and experimental schools should be generalized to all components of the system of alternative schools. Every effective school system needs an increased emphasis on self-direction, a more humane climate, a greater interpenetration of the school and the community, and a sense of teaching as an activity that facilitates learning. Even these themes will be expressed and realized differently in the variety of schools within the system of alternatives.

The concept of alternative schools should not be equated with undue permissiveness or lack of structure in the educational experiences of young people. Some alternative schools will be highly structured, based on considerable external discipline and direction; others will offer students almost complete freedom in their educational tasks. A classical Jesuit school is an alternative to the comprehensive high school just as much as Summerhill is. Educators working in the field of alternative education must not narrowly delimit alternative schools to those institutions that eschew structure and adult direction. Such outré schools form only a minute fraction of the many viable alternative models that are now developing in American secondary education.

The system of alternative schools proposed here should not cost much more than today's comprehensive schools. Careful reallocation of existing resources, accompanied by reappraisal of educational priorities, should pay the bills without undue financial dislocations. Educational planners must not minimize the fundamental changes in structure, organization, methodology, and human interrelationships that a change to alternative schools will require. Moving from a singular to a plural system means a shift in the educational attitudes of everyone, from the classroom teacher to the chief school administrator.

Advantages and Limitations of a System of Alternative Schools

It must be recognized that some of the goals of American secondary education may be achieved more easily by the traditional high school with its variegated student body than by a system of competing alternatives, each of which has a more narrowly based student body. In education as elsewhere, benefits rarely come without costs.

The main advantages and limitations of a change to a system of alternative schools would seem to be the following:

ADVANTAGES

· Alternative programs and schools seriously attempt to individualize education.

· Opportunities are provided for increased community involvement in the operation of schools.

· Students are encouraged to assume greater responsibility for their own education through organizing and managing their individual learning experiences.

· Teachers assume the fully professional roles of diagnosing and prescribing for the individual needs of students.

· Interpersonal relationships between students and teachers are enhanced.

· Differentiated staffing is made possible by team teaching and the use of noncertified personnel as instructional aides.

LIMITATIONS

· Most schools are diffuse in their educational purposes and goals, but alternative schools will have to create an educational rationale if students are to make intelligent choices. This is a hard job, and not every alternative school will be able to do it.

· A significant number of students and their parents, especially those outside the mainstream of middle America, may not have the knowledge or sophistication necessary to make educational choices of this magnitude. The standard secondary school may become by default the custodian of large masses of undirected and uncertain young people, while the more exotic alternatives draw the more able and ambitious.

· Unless vigorous precautions are taken to keep all alternative schools fully representative of the diversity of the population, a system of alternative schools could easily become an apartheid system fractured on lines of race, social caste, economic class, or culture.

Recent Developments

The growth of alternative programs and schools in recent years has been a dramatic response to a miscellany of social problems and forces. School dropouts (or push-outs), philosophical and ideological dissatisfaction with the organizational aridity of existing schools, acute disappointement wth the ends achieved, and deep student estrangement—all these factors have led parents and community groups to seek the creation of alternative schools beyond the control of the dominant system.

The last three years have seen the most explosive growth in the number of alternative programs and schools. The partial success of the earlier programs has had a cumulative effect, and the quest for more satisfying schools seemingly is attracting larger numbers of parents and students.

The trend now seems to be to provide new schools rather than to develop alternative programs within old schools, as was true in the mid-sixties. The June 1972 report of the Educational Research Service shows steadily increasing numbers of alternative schools within public systems.[2]

The *New Schools Exchange* reports the establishment of hundreds of nonpublic alternative schools around the country.[3] It also memorializes their demise when they close for a variety of reasons, the most common being inadequate financial resources. The life of the average free school is estimated at slightly under two years. In spite of repeated failure and endemic bankruptcy, however, new schools continue to open, attesting to the persistence of the idea.

Up to now, alternative learning situations in public and nonpublic schools have been offered only to limited numbers of students. Furthermore, many alternative schools and programs are avowedly experimental. This framework limits their effectiveness. As their efforts prove successful, these programs should be expanded and new variants instituted.

To date, the extension of successful alternative programs

has been relatively infrequent. Indeed, some existing programs and schools are in danger. One of the main reasons for the low survival rate is that the effectiveness of these alternative programs is being assessed by the criteria for conventional school operation rather than by criteria that measure their own objectives. The negative results of such tainted evaluations frequently signal the end of the experiment or cast an unwarranted stigma of failure on what might otherwise be a viable alternative program or school.

An alternative school or program is often established in a desperate attempt to resolve acute problems in the school rather than as an effort to improve educational opportunities. Some of the problems various districts have sought to defuse by alternative approaches are spiraling dropout rates, truancy, pupil control difficulties, drug abuse, pregnancies, and hostilities attendant on racial integration. It is not surprising that few alternative programs or schools can bear this unwieldy burden.

Recommendations to Authorities
Affecting Education at the Secondary Level

Implementing these changes in the secondary structure requires more than the commitment of the local school community and a sprightly educational imagination. Regulations and requirements governing secondary schools must be changed. To this end, the Commission suggests the following steps to be taken by higher authorities:

STATE LEGISLATURES

· State educational funds should be allocated on the basis of the number of school-age children registered within the school, rather than through formulas attached to average daily attendance. The new basis should be average daily membership. Incentives should be included to encourage schools to maintain high standards of average daily attendance. Schools should be able to improve attendance through offering an attractive environment filled with alternatives.

· Mandated lengths for the school year may be eliminated to facilitate "easy entry/easy exit" by the student and to permit mobility within the structure. Mandated length should be eliminated only when school systems can demonstrate increased student performance in less time. Some schools may operate all year, others for a shorter period of time. The length of his personal school year should be one of the options available to each young person at the secondary-school level when he can demonstrate the achievement of performance objectives in less than the prescribed number of days.

· The length of the school day should be varied according to the needs of the individual student. To reimburse the school district on the basis of a six-hour student day is to force every student into the same time framework, whether or not it is appropriate for him.

· Disabling laws establishing the custodial responsibilities of the high schools should be repealed. The courts already have questioned the doctrine of *in loco parentis* in the relationship of the student to the school. Relieving the school of its inappropriate custodial functions will facilitate the use of the community as an extension of the school and permit realization of the open-campus concept.

· Regulations governing teacher certification should be modified to make certain that professional preparation is required only where professional services are involved.

STATE DEPARTMENTS OF EDUCATION

Some states have recently modified their graduation requirements and their criteria for accrediting secondary schools to accommodate alternative schools and programs. An increasing number of state departments of education already permit local districts to convert into Carnegie Units credits earned through independent study and community-based learning.

The Carnegie Unit was established 78 years ago on the basis of a consensus of educators that 120 hours of class time in a year made a significant course. The numbers have inflated since, and now some schools require as much as 180 hours of classroom work for a Carnegie Unit. In the future, credit should be given for independent study through an assessment of individual progress by examination. Anyone completing the objectives of a course should get credit, whether it took him 10 hours or 200 hours.

While new bases for granting credit are already emerging, the Carnegie Unit will remain because many people find comfort and security in the idea that 120 hours of a course will automatically produce a credit. Moreover, the awarding of credits on another basis requires educators to determine the objectives and the outcomes sought in the course. Once that problem is solved, many ways to grant credit become feasible. In practice, the Carnegie Unit is already an excuse rather than a reason for inaction by the schools: a school that really wants to grant credit on other criteria can do so today. But the state departments of education and the accrediting associations should clarify the situation to encourage the timid and reinforce the political position of the bold.

LOCAL BOARDS OF EDUCATION

The decentralized governance of the American schools has been in theory a vast venture into alternative educational programs and schools. Each of the 15,000 school districts in America is, or could be, its own educational laboratory. However, the individual student's options within this national system of alternatives are limited by one intractable constraint— his particular place of residence. A different choice of educational alternatives entails a change of address. People do, in fact, move to put their children in what they consider a desirable school, but the existence of alternatives in the new district is rarely the reason.

In any substantive reform of secondary education the local school board occupies the central role. The cooperation and support of local boards are vital to the creation of alternative schools and programs. The Commission urges each local board of education to take the following actions:

· Each district should provide a broad range of alternative schools and programs so that every student will have meaningful educational options available to him.

· Regulations to prevent racial and socioeconomic segregation in the various alternatives must be established and rigorously enforced.

· Mobility between alternatives should be permitted under controlled conditions, and students should be able to change options without loss of educational pace.

COLLEGES AND UNIVERSITIES

Schools with alternative programs should query the institutions of higher learning that receive most of their graduates to determine whether an unusual secondary-level program will harm the student's chance of being accepted at college. Among the issues that must be resolved are rank in class (which is not only difficult for many alternative programs to compute, but in many cases would pervert their educational goals), nontraditional evaluation procedures, and unusual course and credit designations.

Unfortunately, rank in class is still, in too many instances, a prime criterion for college acceptance. The Commission urges upon colleges and universities the need to develop more reliable, less disruptive indicators of a student's overall high school accomplishment than rank in class and grade-point average, both of which are based upon arbitrary and competitive grades. Other predictors of the student's potential for college work might be more subtle and more difficult to compute, but they would not have such a deleterious effect on the entire secondary school program.

Junior colleges especially will have to provide for graduates of alternative schools who have traveled different educational paths and who will bring unusual strengths and learning approaches to their post-secondary education. Meanwhile, the secondary schools, traditional or otherwise, will have to prepare their graduates for a wide variety of nontraditional college experiences that are now becoming available.

Mention was made in Chapter 7 of the need for high schools to accept work done in college as a valid substitute for high school courses in awarding diplomas. As part of the system of alternatives, full admission to undergraduate programs should be offered to some students in the eleventh and twelfth years. This is not "early admissions," but a redefinition of the process and substance of education beyond the tenth year. Special secondary school/college baccalaureate degree programs should be designed and implemented to apply alternative learning strategies to the problem of articulation between secondary and higher education.

Individual Instruction

The Commission's recommendations for alternative programs and schools are student-oriented and assume that once an individual's needs are determined, instruction can be largely student-directed and student-administered.

Individualized instruction has been a watchword of educational consultants and spokesmen for years. Little evidence can be found of its effective utilization on any broad scale. On the contrary, as the high school has grown larger, attention to individuals has diminished. Alternative programs are not all things to all adolescents. Such programs can produce better student-teacher rapport through any of four basic approaches to individualized instruction:

· *Individually Diagnosed and Prescribed Instruction:* School personnel select materials and determine learning objectives, and each student progresses at his own rate.

· *Self-directed Instruction:* School personnel determine the learning objectives and each student chooses his own materials and how he wants to work.

· *Personalized Instruction Programs:* The student establishes his own objectives but must then follow a program established by the teacher and use materials selected by school personnel.

· *Independent Study Programs:* The student establishes his own objectives, selects materials, and determines procedures.

Alternative programs and schools seek to incorporate all the tenets of individualization. They are approaches to providing better education for a greater variety of students.

NOTES

1. Stephen K. Bailey, Francis U. Macy, and Donn F. Vickers, *Alternative Paths to the High School Diploma,* prepared by the Policy Institute, Syracuse University Research Corporation, for the Ford Foundation, Mar. 1, 1973.

2. *Alternative High Schools: Some Pioneer Programs,* Educational Research Service, Circular No. 4, Washington, D.C., 1972.

3. "Projections for the Free Schools Movement: Part I," *New Schools Exchange Newsletter,* Issue No. 51, Santa Barbara, Calif., n.d., p. 9.

PART V

THE CHALLENGE: CRISIS AND CHANGE IN SECONDARY EDUCATION

CHAPTER 10

The Crisis in School Security

Recommendation No. 21: Planning for School Security
*All secondary school systems should develop security plans
to safeguard students, faculty, equipment, and facilities. Specific procedures must be developed for faculty members to
follow in case of disruption.*

Recommendation No. 22: Records of Violence
*State legislation should be enacted to require principals to
file a detailed report on all serious assaults within schools. The
information contained should form a data base from which
security personnel could identify potential trouble areas and
move to alleviate future problems.*

Crime in the high schools, unheard of only a few years ago,
has become an inescapable aspect of the need for reform.
Perspective on the problem only makes it worse. Adolescence
has always been the age of the highest incidence of criminal
activity, and schoolyards have always been the scene of much
random fighting. However, the difference between a fight and
an assault is real, and it is a difference in kind, not just in
degree. In the toughest neighborhoods school used to be a

sanctuary from violence, a place where fights were broken up. Now, assaults on students and teachers by other students have become part of the environment of education.

Every student has the right to attend school without fear for his physical well-being. Nobody would dream of denying the existence of this right; but nobody is doing much to defend it.

A brief examination of recent incidents indicates the seriousness of the threat. At Jefferson High School in Los Angeles, homecoming activities included the shooting of five youths, and this is only one of sixty recent incidents involving guns in Los Angeles schools. In Atlanta, a twelve-year-old boy who was being teased by classmates pulled a hand gun from his pocket and opened fire on his tormentors. The ensuing investigation resulted in the confiscation of fifteen hand guns from students. Five youths were wounded in racial violence at a central high school in Pontiac, Michigan. Chicago recently reported fifteen school incidents involving weapons; Kansas City reported sixteen. The problem is current, important, and worsening. It is nationwide and exists at both urban and suburban schools.

Opinions on the causes vary widely: Philip Viso, principal of the Industrial Skill Center in Chicago, one of the nation's most successful vocational schools, places the blame on the school itself. He contends that the central problem is a lack of substance and meaning in the classroom, which makes wandering in the hall or shooting craps in the rest room a more attractive option for students. He gives his educational program the credit for the absence of violent incidents at his school: "School attendance should come from a personal desire, so it is a matter of program design. The law will never compel compulsory thinking, only 'body in place.'"

Stephen K. Bailey, who headed a major study of school disruption for the U.S. Office of Education and the Syracuse University Research Corporation, argues that much of the blame lies on the communty as a whole: "Any society with social injustices is going to have problems with domestic tranquillity. Every philosophy since Plato's has said this." Bailey suggests fresh analyses of both the in-school and the out-of-school causes of disruption.

One of the nation's most effective school security chiefs, Edward D. Brady of Chicago, contends that failure to report incidents is at the heart of the trouble: "Unless you know the scope of the problem, you are not going to solve it."

School principals seem to feel that the disclosure of an assault is a reflection on the school. Consequently, most incidents of crime in schools are handled by the principal within the walls, and are never reported. There is reason to believe that fewer than 10 percent of crimes committed in school buildings, including violent crimes, are divulged. Statistics from one city will show hundreds of incidents in a given year, while those from another city of comparable size and similar population show no more than four or five. The statistics reflect the policies of school systems, not the incidence of crime.

Most school boards do not require the maintenance of detailed records of violent incidents. Indeed, principals are often encouraged to pretend it never happened. Many schools have a policy of sending any injured child to the hospital in a teacher's car, because a call for an ambulance would trigger an official record. As the late Senator Thomas Dodd commented to the Senate subcommittee on juvenile delinquency, "It is in the interest of the system that whatever untoward violence occurs be hushed up. It reflects on the school system itself." Historically, there was something to be said for the tradition that school principals settled issues privately with the student, parent, and teacher. Today, there is no justification for it.

Schools should be required to maintain a running account of incidents by category and to report them weekly to the superintendent's office. The superintendent, on his part, should be obliged to report all violent incidents to the school board.

The reaction of the Commission to the extent and seriousness of crimes in schools is evident in this report. No one can underestimate the problem. At the same time the "criminals" in these cases are our students and are juveniles. This report cannot be construed to encourage a process of harsh vindictiveness, nor can it suggest that schools become a special arm of the criminal justice system. What it does insist upon is that educators share with families, communities, and youths themselves responsibility for maintaining the teaching-learning process in a crimeless and fearless atmosphere.

While school officials should retain their authority to handle petty offenses by children through an administrative process, their obligations to the school as a society and to the total community transcend their obligations to the individual student when a crime has been committed. Assault with a deadly weapon, felonious assult, patterns of systematic intimidation that give children a rational fear of coming to school—such conduct must be dealt with in the criminal justice system, not in school. The criminal justice system must live up to its responsibilities. Too many district attorneys feel they have better things to do; too many juvenile court judges act as advocates for young criminals rather than protectors of the school community.

An assault in school must not be treated like a casual fight, as a discipline problem to be solved by hasty (and often inappropriate) punishment meted out by busy school personnel. This is a matter for the courts, and published school policy—if necessary, state legislation—must say so. Crimes committed in school are just as serious as crimes committed on the streets and should be dealt with accordingly by the district attorney.

Victims have rights, too. Where there is a clash of rights, a civilized community will give priority to the victim's rights.

In 1970, 682 large urban secondary schools were surveyed in a national study of *Disruption in Urban Public Secondary Schools,* sponsored by the National Association of Secondary School Principals. Among the major conclusions were the following:

· The size of the student body is a more important variable than the size of the city in which a school is located.

· Disruption is positively related to integration. Schools which are almost all white or all black are less likely to be disrupted.

· Integrated schools with higher percentages of black students are less likely to be disrupted if such schools also have high percentages of black staff.

· Disruption and average daily attendance are directly related. Where average daily attendance is lower, disruption is higher and vice versa.[1]

Another aspect of school security—or insecurity—is vandalism. The best estimate is that public education spends over $150 million per year to repair such damages. A Boston study reported that cost of vandalism in that city ran as high as $10.79 per pupil. Even the lightly treated prank of bomb threats costs taxpayers an average of $2,000 per threat.

The Schools' Rest Rooms

State laws prohibiting minors from purchasing cigarettes make enormous problems for the schools. Most state laws do not forbid young people to smoke—just to buy cigarettes. There is not even a pretense of enforcement of this legislation: all fifty states permit unmonitored vending machines from which anyone can purchase cigarettes.

Because state statutes forbid selling cigarettes to minors, schools consider themselves bound to prevent smoking by students. Unfortunately, most schools have no control over what happens in the rest rooms. The consequence is that students who have acquired the smoking habit congregate in rest rooms. When nonsmoking students attempt to use these facilities, they find them unpleasantly filled with smoke. Furthermore, nonsmoking students may be confronted by cliques of smokers who indulge in extortion and harrassment of their peers.

A dozen or so rest rooms scattered around a school plant are difficult to monitor. Most schools have simply given up on the problem and ignore it. This Commission cannot ignore it. As a first step, the Commission proposes that state legislatures repeal their ineffective laws against smoking by adolescents and that schools provide smoking areas for students similar to those provided for teachers. It is absolutely essential that the rest rooms of the nation's schools be kept clean and safe for the benefit of all students.

In many desegregated schools, both male and female students of both races are literally petrified at the thought of having to use the school's rest rooms. These facilities have become turfs where gangs of both majority and minority students concentrate, and waylay other students who come in. Crime is rampant in the washrooms.

The problem is far more serious for girls than for boys. It is a very easy matter for a group to snatch a girl's pocketbook, block off the Kotex machine, threaten to burn her hair, or molest her in other ways. In its investigation of this situation, Commission members received such reports as:

[From a male senior] I haven't been in the rest room in this school in four years. I was attacked in there as a freshman and have been afraid to go back.

[From a female senior] I use the rest room in the filling station across the street because a gang burned my hair and took my pocketbook in the girls' rest room.

To determine the depth of the problem of violence in the schools, the Commission polled its national panel of secondary school students:

• 93 percent of the respondents indicated an appalling degree of smoking, use of drugs, and gambling in the rest rooms in their schools.

• 41 percent of the respondents said that students are sometimes attacked and beaten up in rest rooms in their schools.

• 35 percent of the respondents reported that students are robbed in the rest rooms of their schools.

• 95 percent of the respondents indicated that students congregate and loiter in the rest rooms of their schools.

• 78 percent of the respondents reported that some students in their schools refuse to use the rest rooms.

• 41 percent of the respondents indicated that no organized efforts have been made in their schools to control what happens in the rest rooms.

The rest room situation is intolerable and must be remedied. It is not enough to lock the more isolated rest rooms in the school plant and occasionally patrol the others. The following procedures seem promising to the Commission:

• Close the special rest rooms for teachers and require teachers to use the same rest rooms as the students. Fifty-two percent of the Commission's panel thought this would be a good idea; many respondents reported that their rest rooms already serve both students and teachers.

• Permit smoking by students in specified areas that are not demeaning, conspicuous by their location, or unusable during inclement weather. While this suggestion is made regretfully, because the Commission accepts the Surgeon General's finding that cigarettes are harmful to health, there appears to be no alternative. Nearly all schools provide smoking areas for teachers and this double standard is one of the problems. Ninety percent of the Commission's panel agreed on the need for official smoking rooms. In the free response section of the questionnaire, most students reported that smoking was by far the most common abuse of the rest room.

· New schools should avoid the aggregate toilet designs which are universal. Individual rest rooms leading off the main corridor should be provided. This is admittedly a drastic and expensive solution: seventy-three percent of the student panel thought it too costly in space and construction money.

· Provide direct supervision of the rest rooms by staffing them. Both the panel (90 percent) and the Commission reject the installation of electronic monitoring devices as a serious invasion of privacy.

· Involve responsible student groups in patrolling and supervising these facilities.

Police in the Schools

Attempting to cope with violence, many school boards have begun to employ people to perform police functions within the schools. In 1969, a newspaper of the educational field described the situation as follows:

> Police patrols are now common in the corridors of our urban schools. Security guards are stationed in every junior and senior high school in New York City. The Newark schools now maintain a security force larger than the police force of many New Jersey communities.[2]

Strong-arm techniques alone will never restore order to terror-ridden schools. "Educators believe that the police can prevent violence," Major Tyree S. Broomfield, director of conflict management for the Dayton, Ohio, police department, told a meeting in Washington in early 1973. "They cannot. They react to violence. Once in a school, we assume the kids are wrong and proceed on that premise. Once in, it is very hard to get us out."[3]

School principals must learn how to work with the police, how to deploy them, and how to disengage them from the school. Sociologist S. D. Vestermark, Jr., told the Commission that "most principals in my experience simply do not understand that there are, in fact, command procedures for calling, using, and deploying the police in a school situation."

The use of uniformed policemen in the schools should be limited to special or emergency situations and police should be restricted to carefully defined roles worked out in advance with local law enforcement officials. In fact, all aspects of a school's reaction to disruption should be planned in advance, and everyone on the staff should know what is expected of him in any such situation. As little as possible should be left to improvisation or to chance.

Many schools now refuse to cooperate with law enforcement personnel who wish to interrogate a student at school. Such policies are untenable: school personnel must cooperate with the local police in the performance of their duties. However, a member of the school's staff should be present at any interview on school property to ensure that the student's rights are protected and to serve as an objective witness. When possible, school personnel should notify the student's parents prior to the interrogation.

The Teacher's Position

Maintaining order on school property has traditionally been part of a teacher's normal duties. Because of the increase in physical assaults in recent years, many teachers are afraid of students and have turned over their role in school discipline to building administrators and school security officers. The growing student control problem is reflected in the greater number of men being hired as teachers at the secondary level.

Many observers argue that teachers have purposely used the cloak of professionalism and the muscle of collective bargaining to evade what should be their responsibilties for discipline throughout the school. Dennis Jaffe, a drug education expert, believes that teachers are the best resource for controlling student behavior—provided they are willing to work with the students instead of just teaching at them. Jaffe has also called for the allocation of some security money to train students to assume school-level responsibilities and put them in closer contact with school authorities.

Obviously, there is no way teachers can escape involvement in this problem. Classrooms cannot long be safe in a school where the halls and rest rooms are dangerous, and students who are concerned about their personal safety after the bell rings are not likely to concentrate on their work in class.

Expanding the School Campus

In 1970, following a study of 110 urban school districts, the Senate Subcommittee to Investigate Juvenile Delinquency reported that student assaults on teachers had increased 612 percent. These figures are now obsolete; things are worse.

Assaults on students have been increasing at an even more rapid rate and trouble the Commission even more. Only the deeply psychotic student can fail to know that an assault on a teacher is dangerous. Whatever the policy of the school board or the principal, an attack on a teacher will be news; the police will not only be informed, they will be egged on by editorials. By contrast, assaults on and robberies of students must seem quite safe in an appalling number of schools. Victim, principal, superintendent, even school board member will each, for his own reason, be afraid to report the incident. The Commission insists that this cycle of fears be broken, so that schools and students can go about their business in peace. The Commission is convinced that the increasing size of high schools is part of the problem. One step that could be taken immediately is for the outsize high schools to organize away from bigness. Costs outweigh benefits whenever a school grows to the point of fostering anonymity. Some reduction can be accomplished, in effect, through adoption of the "house" organization of the high school, which gives both teachers and students a manageably small target for the direction of collegial loyalties.

Alternative programs using the entire community as the school campus, coupled with a vast expansion of work-study opportunities, would guarantee better dispersal of students. Quite apart from their educational value, action-learning programs pursued in the community would diminish the severity of the school crime problem. Again, the key is community involvement; and again, this involvement must include the use of all community resources as the high school's campus.

NOTES

1. Stephen K. Bailey, *Disruption in Urban Public Secondary Schools* (Washington, D.C.: National Association of Secondary School Principals, n.d.), pp. 10–12.

2. "The Character of High School Protests," *Education Daily*, vol. 2, no. 111, June 11, 1969, p. 5.

3. Remarks made by T. S. Broomfield at the School Safety Conference sponsored by the U.S. Office of Education in Washington, D.C., on Jan. 29–30, 1973.

CHAPTER 11

Student Rights
and Obligations:
The Need for Balance

Recommendation No. 23: Code of Student Rights and Obligations

Every secondary school should develop and adopt a code of student rights and obligations. This code should be published and distributed to every student. It should include all school rules, regulations, and procedures for suspension and expulsion with explanations of how students can defend themselves through established process.

Recommendation No. 24: School Newspapers

A school newspaper is a house organ which is operated, financed, and therefore controlled by the school system, which may be legally liable for its contents. In cases where students and school administrators become deadlocked over censorship, a faculty-community-student committee should decide the issue. Some schools may find it necessary to withdraw financial support allowing students complete freedom of ex-

pression in what would then be entirely their own publication, with a corresponding liability for what is printed.

Recommendation No. 25: Right of Privacy

A student's school records must contain only factual information necessary to the educative process. The entire file must be available at all times for review by students and their parents but must not be accessible to "persons not in interest." Records should be forwarded to another school system, university, or prospective employer only at the written request of the student, his parents, or the receiving school.

That part of a student's records which pertain to his mental health should contain only entries made under the direction of the student's physician and must be kept separately from his academic records. The complete record or any of its contents should be released only to the student, his parents, or to his physician at the student's or parent's request.

Recommendation No. 26: Corporal Punishment

Several states have outlawed corporal punishment with no resulting loss in control or authority. Corporal punishment should be abolished by statute in all states. In the modern world, corporal punishment is necessarily "cruel and unusual."

Recommendation No. 27: Student Activities

Scholarship should not be a requisite for participation in sports, band, singing, cheerleading, or other student activities important to the social development of adolescents. Neither the local school nor state activities associations should establish scholarship standards. Any student in good standing in a school should have the right to participate in any of the school's activities with the exception of honor societies specifically established to reward scholarship.

Recommendation No. 28: Compulsory Attendance

If the high school is not to be a custodial institution, the

*state must not force adolescents to attend. Earlier maturity—
physical, sexual, and intellectual—requires an option of earlier
departure from the restraints of formal schooling.*

*The formal school-leaving age should be dropped to age
fourteen. Other programs should accommodate those who
wish to leave school, and employment laws should be rewritten to assure on-the-job training in full-time service and work.*

Recommendation No. 29: Free K-14 Public Education

*The Congress of the United States in conjunction with state
legislatures should enact legislation that will entitle each citizen
to fourteen years of tuition-free education beyond kindergarten, only eight of which would be compulsory. The remaining six years should be available for use by anyone at any
stage of his life. Congressional involvement is essential to
assure equal access in an age of interstate mobility.*

Recommendation No. 30: Youth Organizations

*The National Association of Secondary School Principals,
a professional organization for school administrators, currently
operates two of the largest organizations affecting public high
school youth: the National Student Council Association and
the National Honor Society. The principals' group should dissociate itself from these organizations and help them become
independent national youth organizations.*

The Rights of Students

The issue of students' rights, privileges, and responsibilities
is almost as old as the country itself. In 1825, Thomas Jefferson complained about a group of students at the University
of Virginia who, "animated first with wine," assaulted some
professors, thereby weakening Jefferson's hope that "much of
self-government might be trusted to the discretion of the
students of the age of 16 and upwards. . . ."[1] For the past

decade, educators have been forcefully confronted with Jefferson's question: How much self-government can be entrusted to students? Like Jefferson, many of them are disappointed; but in many cases their disappointment fulfills their prophecy, and a disinterested observer might feel they protest too much.

Until the late 1960s high school students had few rights at school other than those that could be enforced by influential parents. Administrators and teachers enjoyed a wide range of discretion in student discipline and control under the doctrine of *in loco parentis*. School officials were parental surrogates as long as adolescents were in school. However, while parents are mostly informal in exercising authority over their children, schools need organization. With the passage of time, school organization became a set of rules by which large numbers of adolescents could be controlled by a few adults.

In 1969 the Danforth and Ford Foundations sponsored a study of the political environment inside schools, and one of the reports dealt with student rights:

> Due process is not available to students. When students are accused by teachers of violations of school rules, they already stand convicted. There is no presumption of innocence until evidence is heard. No witnesses are called; no opportunity is afforded the student to defend himself. The administration and the teaching faculty of a school form a united front to maintain control, and a principal, even when he suspects the teacher is wrong, is more likely to take the side of the teacher than that of the student.[2]

The authority of educators to punish students in school was not seriously questioned until February 1969, when the United States Supreme Court ruled against the Des Moines school district in the now famous *Tinker* case. The question was the right of students to wear arm bands at school to protest the Vietnam war. The Court went beyond the matter of arm bands and ruled that children in school have the same constitutional rights as adults in the outside world. Associate Justice Abe Fortas wrote in the Court's decision:

> It can hardly be argued that either students or teachers shed their constitutional rights to freedom of speech or expression at the schoolhouse gate. This has been the unmistakable holding of this Court for almost 50 years. . . .
>
> . . . Students in school as well as out of school are "persons" under our Constitution. They are possessed of fundamental rights which the State must respect, just as they themselves must respect their obligations to the State. . . .[3]

Prior to *Tinker,* few school administrators and teachers could have imagined that children in school were persons under the Constitution: the Constitution was for those over twenty-one. Since *Tinker,* literally hundreds of court cases have elaborated the rights of students in such matters as length of hair, mustaches, beards, dress, the wearing of buttons, distribution of literature, freedom of expression, freedom of assembly, freedom of student newspapers to reflect the judgment of student editors, and, more recently, due process.

In 1969, when student disruptions were making headlines across the nation, there were nearly 500 underground high school papers, and not far from 500 ongoing attempts to stop them. A number of court cases ruled in favor of students' rights to carry and distribute literature, but the courts did not completely deny discretion to school officials. In *Eisner v. The Stamford Board of Education,* the Court of Appeals for the Second Circuit upheld the school board's power to insist that all materials distributed on school property be submitted beforehand to the school principal. However, the specific rules written by the school board were declared unconstitutional. The regulations had not specified the manner of submission, the exact party to whom the material must be submitted, or the time within which a decision must be rendered; and they had not provided for a hearing or for appeal.

The Court's opinion illustrates the administrator's dilemma:

> The risk taken if a few students abuse their First Amendment rights of free speech and press is outweighed by the far greater risk run by suppressing free speech and press among the young. The remedy for today's alienation and disorder among the young is not less but more free expression of ideas. In part, the First Amendment acts as a "safety valve" and tends to decrease the resort to violence by frustrated citizens. Student newspapers are valuable educational tools, and also serve to aid school administrators by providing them with an insight into student thinking and student problems. They are valuable peaceful channels of student protest which should be encouraged, not suppressed.[4]

School administrators or school boards who deny freedom of speech or of the student press will be at a great disadvantage legally if taken to court—and students disgruntled enough to start an underground newspaper are keenly aware that the Bill of Rights applies to them, too. School personnel do not have absolute authority over students: they must restrain their conduct within constitutional limits.

Nevertheless, every official school newspaper which receives an operating subsidy from the school is necessarily to some extent a house organ. Legally, the school system is liable for its contents, and will have to pay at least legal costs and sometimes damages if the paper prints anything that is actionable. Courts will sustain self-protection by the school in this area. Perhaps the best compromise is a policy which permits student editors to appeal censorship by administrators to a faculty-community committee. If the student editors are not willing to accept this degree of control, they should put out their paper entirely on their own, without subsidy from the school budget.

Following an extended dispute over the publication of two controversial articles in a subsidized student paper, the school board in Lynbrook, New York, established the following editorial policy:

> Articles will be restrained by the editors and the paper's advisor on the legal basis of libel, privacy, contempt, obscenity, and copyright. The advisor . . . also maintains the right to withhold articles on the grounds of good taste and in accordance with school policies.[5]

DUE PROCESS

Due process is the most complicated of the newly won rights of students in school, because nobody knows exactly what due process is. One Supreme Court decision described it as "an elusive concept. Its exact boundaries are undefinable, and its content varies according to specific factual contexts. . . ."[6] Another decision held that "the touchstones of the application of due process are reasonableness and fairness in view of all the facts and circumstances of the particular case. . . ."[7] This helps a little, but not much.

The matter of administrative due process in school discipline cases is even more complicated than due process in criminal matters. No doubt the requirements are less; but how much less, nobody knows. There are centuries of precedent to cite when considering due process in the courts, but administrative due process is new.

The most detailed statement of the requirements for due process in cases involving student suspension or expulsion was written in a recent federal district decision:

1. Written notice to parents and student including a specific statement of the charges which, if proved, would justify the punishment sought.

2. A full hearing after adequate notice.

3. An impartial tribunal with the authority to examine exhibits and other evidence against the student.

4. Representation by legal counsel (though not at public expense).

5. Confrontation and examination of adverse witnesses.

6. Presentation of evidence on behalf of the student.

7. Access by all parties to a record of the proceedings.

8. The requirement that the decision of the authorities be based upon substantial evidence.[8]

Higher courts may ultimately decide that school personnel simply do not have time for so complete a panoply of due process. However, there can be no doubt that most of the expansion of student rights in the last few years will be permanent. Students are persons under the Constitution, and the ground rules for schools that were enforceable under the doctrine of *in loco parentis* can survive only if nobody challenges them.

COMPULSORY SCHOOLING

To the rights the courts have already secured for American students, the Commission would like to add another: the right not to be in formal school beyond the age of fourteen. Compulsory attendance laws are the dead hand on the high schools. The liberation of youth and the many freedoms which the courts have given to students within the last decade make it impossible for the school to continue as a custodial institution and also to perform effectively as a teaching institution. The harm done to the school by the student who does not want to be there is measured not only by the incidence of vandalism and assault but also by a subtle and continuous degradation of the tone of the educational enterprise.

There is some question as to whether compulsory attendance in the secondary school can survive constitutional challenge. In 1972 the Supreme Court struck down that part of the Wisconsin law which compelled children of members of the Amish religion to attend school beyond the eighth grade. Chief Justice Burger wrote:

The requirement for compulsory education beyond the eighth grade is a relatively recent development in our

history. Less than 60 years ago, the educational requirements of almost all of the States were satisfied by completion of the elementary grades, at least where the child
was regularly and lawfully employed. . . .

. . . The origins of the requirement for school attendance
to age 16, an age falling after the completion of elementary school but before completion of high school, are
not entirely clear. But to some extent such laws reflected
the movement to prohibit most child labor under age 16
that culminated in the provisions of the Federal Fair
Labor Standards Act of 1938. . . .

The requirement of compulsory schooling to age 16 must
therefore be viewed as aimed not merely at providing
educational opportunities for children, but as an alternative to the equally undesirable consequence of unhealth-
ful child labor displacing adult workers, or, on the other
hand, forced idleness. The two kinds of statutes—compulsory school attendance and child labor laws—tend to
keep children of certain ages off the labor market and
in the school. . . .[9]

If Amish children cannot be compelled to go to school, it
is hard to see how others can be under a rule of law that
promises equal treatment to all.

If compulsory attendance worked—if it actually forced
everyone into school, and the school taught them something
important when they came—a case could be made for seeking
to preserve it, even at the cost of some disruption in the
school. However, the law is not effective. In many inner city
schools average daily attendance runs less than 50 percent
of the register.

Tragically, these are the students who most need help in
school. Data from the National Assessment project reveal that
achievement in the schools of the inner city has fallen below
that in the rural South, which traditionally brought up the
rear of American education. The low attendance rates and
low achievement of the inner city are artifacts of the present
legal situation which theoretically compels attendance. More

of the same will not make better. Enforcement of these laws is certain to become even more of a joke if the school systems succeed in their campaign to persuade state legislatures to calculate school aid on the basis of membership rather than average daily attendance.

The nation does not need laws that force adolescents to go to school. It needs schools and school-related programs that make adolescents wish to come.

Society must not require the high school to be the institution that keeps adolescents off the street for six or seven hours a day; the high school has more important work to do. On the other hand, a society must remain concerned over its young adolescents. While compulsory attendance should be abandoned, compulsory education which prepares each youngster for adult living should continue. In other words, students do not have to go to the traditional high school and just sit in attendance, but they should still be required to acquire competencies for adult living. The public is weary of footing welfare bills because adolescents are unable to get jobs. No matter where or how they attend school, they should develop competencies.

It is by no means established that dropouts must be losers. A report from the Institute for Social Research of the University of Michigan claims that "shortening the prescribed minimum period of full-time uninterrupted schooling might be a positive step toward new patterns of lifetime education in which individuals can choose for themselves among a wide range of 'educational life-styles.' "[10]

The Commission was deeply troubled about some of the implications of its recommendation of an end to compulsory attendance beyond the age of fourteen. Even the present situation is preferable to complete abandonment of what is likely to be the unluckiest segment of the adolescent population. The reduction of compulsory attendance laws to age fourteen must follow, not precede, the change in laws which will provide school-leaving youth real alternatives for employment or an alternative mode of education. This recommendation should in no way be considered a convenient way to "push out" unwanted youth, especially those from disadvantaged urban areas and minority families.

Public policy and programs must accommodate adolescents from fourteen years of age upward in both part-time and full-time jobs. Occupational educational programs must be established to permit on-the-job training for every employed adolescent, at least up to the age previously set as the minimum school-leaving age. The change in the law should not be seen as a way to cut the education budget; at least as much money should be spent on the education of these children out of school as would have been spent had they remained in school.

While urging a cut-off on compulsory schooling after the eighth grade, the Commission proposes that the right to free public education be expanded to cover fourteen rather than twelve years, and that two years of education beyond the high school be made available to all Americans, both adolescents and adults. This is to be an entitlement: anyone who has not yet had fourteen years of education at state expense will have the right to go to the schools and colleges of his state and demand admission to a program suited to his needs and abilities. Taken together, the two recommendations establish a system in which an individual can drop out of formal education when he deems it appropriate to do so, and reenter at his convenience at any time during his lifetime, even as a senior citizen. The Commission expects that employers would then help their employees return to school or college at those points in their careers where additional formal education would be most useful to them, and that many more people would do so once the barrier of cost was removed.

Carrying out this recommendation will require action by all the state legislatures, and also by Congress, to make sure that opportunities are equalized and interstate mobility is not discouraged.

Student Obligations

The schools have been agitated now for eight years over the question of student rights, but there has been no corresponding hue and cry about the equally important matter of student obligations. Within the last several years many states, most high schools, and dozens of outside organizations have published manuals entitled "Student Rights and Responsibilities." About 99 percent of the content of these documents deals with student rights, and about 1 percent with responsibilities. Even if the balance were better, the words used betray an imbalance. "Rights" are enforceable; "responsibilities" are not. In dealing with the other side of the shield of "rights," the Commission chooses the word "obligations." The same people who will "shirk their responsibilities" will "live up to their obligations." The Commission expects students endowed with rights to live up to their obligations.

The lowering of the legal age to eighteen in 1971 brought with it emancipation for young people on a broad front. Many states have now extended all of the rights of majority to young people in this age bracket. A natural outgrowth is a new insistence by both the legal and political systems that eighteen-year-olds accept full liability for their actions. In the past, adolescents were treated as a privileged caste and their sanctuary was vigorously defended by their parents, the schools, and the law. The consequence was failure to learn that in the real world people pay for what they break.

Many people feel that the courts have been overly liberal with student rights and careless about student obligations, but an examination of the decisions themselves shows that the judges have worked to find a tenable balance. The courts are petitioned, of course, to enforce rights rather than obligations, but even when the students are the winners, the courts will usually add a balancing phrase. Thus, the Supreme Court held in *Tinker* that students "are possessed of fundamental rights which the State must respect, *just as they themselves must respect their obligations to the State....*"[11]

Among the efforts to make adolescents under eighteen more mindful of their obligations is a national movement to compel parents to fulfill their parental duties. Camden, New Jersey, recently enacted what is probably the nation's strongest assertion of the accountability of parents. Among other things, the Camden ordinance outlines parental duties related to supervision of children and adolescents, and assesses a $500 fine or ninety days in jail for parents who fail to supervise a minor child under the age of eighteen. Supervision is defined in the city ordinance as "the exercise of control over a minor child, knowing his whereabouts, knowing with whom he associates and in what activities he or she may engage which could affect or offend the public peace, safety and morals."[12]

It is indeed essential, though not within the purview of this Commission, that parents accept and carry out their obligations to their children, and schools should exert what influence they may have to improve the performance of parents.

Within the high school, the first step toward making students recognize their obligations is to state them, in clear, unequivocal language. A list of student obligations should be developed at the building or district level by a student-parent-faculty-administrator committee. This code should be posted, published, and distributed to every student. The discussion about student rights and obligations is incomplete without a consideration of the process by which a student is involved in the determination of both his rights and obligations. There will be fewer violations of school rules and regulations when students have a regular procedure for input into the determination of those rules and regulations.

The liability of students and the obligations of the schools form a two-way street. In the terms of the goals of education stated earlier in these pages, the schools have undertaken obligations to teach everyone to read and write and figure and manage their own political and ecological roles. To some extent, it is the inability of the schools to completely fulfill their obligations that has provoked the students to neglect theirs.

The schools must make a mighty effort to align their programs realistically with the development of new knowledge and the increased sophistication which students bring to the school's marketplace. Students, on their part, must act responsibly and seriously while in the environment of the school. The schoolhouse is no place for caprice and undisciplined individuals.

The Commission recommends a new obligation relating to the new right of fourteen years of free schooling. In return for this commitment by the state, it is proposed that all adolescents and adults who are attending schools and free colleges either donate the equivalent of a month's community service for each year above twelve or be required to pay a nominal tuition fee. Among the ways this service could be performed is by work in the conservation of water and soil and wilderness. Dr. George Gallup reports that a large majority of the American public supports the idea of a youth conservation corps, modeled on the civilian conservation camps of the thirties. Work in such camps could bring together students who are giving a month's service and dropouts who have come to the camps for a more extended stay. Of teen-agers from poverty areas not in school, a recent Labor Department study showed unemployment rates of 18.1 percent among whites and 44.9 percent among blacks. The provision of conservation camps and service programs would be a sensible alternative to schools they do not wish to attend and jobs they cannot get.

Corporal Punishment

Among the urgent side issues raised in the discussion of student rights is the question of corporal punishment. Children and youth in school are the only members of society to whom physical punishment can be legally administered without court procedure. Neither the military nor the penitentiary employ physical punishment, except in the prisons of the state of Mississippi. According to the National Education Association, thirteen states have laws on the books condoning physical punishment in school while only three states have laws expressly forbidding the use of corporal punishment.

This is not a recent phenomenon. As far back as 1853 the Supreme Court of Indiana wrote:

> The public seems to cling to the despotism in the government of schools which has been discarded everywhere else. . . . The husband can no longer moderately chastise his wife; nor . . . the master his servant or apprentice. Even the degrading cruelties of the naval service have been arrested. Why the person of the schoolboy . . . should be less sacred in the eye of the law than that of the apprentice or the sailor is not easily explained.[13]

In 1971, the United States Supreme Court refused to hear an appeal from a lower court ruling which had upheld the authority of the Dallas school system to administer physical punishment.[14] In response, a National Committee to Abolish Corporal Punishment in Schools was formed, sponsored initially by the American Civil Liberties Union and the American Orthopsychiatric Association. This committee supported an investigation into the Dallas situation which found that 24,350 paddlings were administered in Dallas schools during the 1971–72 school year. The superintendent of schools confirmed the statistics.

A few states have passed legislation forbidding corporal punishment in schools. All should do so. The administering of physical punishment is demeaning to an institution which claims to be making human society more humane. As a corrective force, the act of paddling is at best a clumsy and unreliable instrument.

The administration of physical pain as ·a method of maintaining discipline has been abandoned by the military and the penal systems. It is now time for the public schools to cease using the instrument of physical punishment as a means for maintaining discipline.

School Records

In the course of their investigations, subcommittee members of the Commission were appalled at the looseness with which many schools handle student records and their neglect of students' right to privacy. The most frequent violation of this right occurs as part of research projects. University professors, governmental agencies, even market researchers are given access to student records. Revealing to outsiders the information in student records is an unacceptable breach of each individual's right to privacy.

School records are items of personal history that may be extremely important to the person involved. They contain subject grades, reports of discipline infractions and activity participation, comments by teachers, IQ test scores, achievement test scores, psychological reports, medical histories, and evaluations by educators.

In 1970, the Russell Sage Foundation issued guidelines for the collection, maintenance, and dissemination of student records. The central statements of the report were these:

1. The collection and maintenance of any information about a pupil or his family constitutes a potential intrusion on privacy.
2. We urge school authorities to begin from the fundamental principle that no information should be collected

from students without the prior informed consent of the child and his parents.

3. Periodically, parents should be informed of the content of these records and their right of access to this data.[15]

The most controversial of the Russell Sage recommendations is the right of access. The Commission concurs with the recommendation that each adolescent and his parents have an absolute right to see what has been filed under this adolescent's name. An "interpretation" of the record by school officials does not meet the need. Both parents and adolescents have the right to inspect the record itself in its entirety.

Records should contain only what is necessary for the school to know. They should be forwarded to another school system, university, or prospective employer only at the written request of the student, his parents, or the receiving school. Mental health records should be kept separate from other records and should contain only entries made under the direction of the student's personal physician. These records should be released only to the student, his parents, or to his physician at the student's or parent's request.

COMPUTER BANKS OF STUDENT RECORDS

When a new student enrolls in a high school it may take weeks—even months—to obtain his "cumulative file" from his former school. In this highly mobile society, unconscionable delays in transferring records have produced a demand for a national computer system that would give access to a student's record within twenty-four hours.

The U.S. Office of Education is currently supporting a national computer bank for the children of migrant parents, and USOE officials estimate that between 75 and 85 percent of all migrant children's records are now in the memory core of a computerized student information system located at the University of Arkansas. Military officials who are responsible for the Department of Defense dependents' schools have expressed an interest in setting up a computer system to house data on military dependents who change schools frequently. Educational computer enthusiasts are pressing for a national data bank for all student records.

Computer data banks pose special problems of maintenance, security, and access; the possibility of their misuse is a potential infringement of the constitutional rights of individuals. Efforts in this direction should proceed only with great caution, and the major concern of the programmers should not be the system and the computer but the right of privacy.

The Commission urges strongly against allowing students' personal and private school records to be computerized in a national center. If records are computerized, the bank should be retained in the school district with safeguards to assure the students' right of privacy. There should be no regional or national computer bank of student records, however convenient such a system might be for the schools.

National Organizations Which Serve High School Youth

Two national organizations influence the lives of high school students: the National Association of Student Councils, which reports a membership of approximately 4,800 schools; and the National Honor Society, with affiliates in 18,000 schools. Both the organizations are operated by the National Association of Secondary School Principals and have their headquarters in the Reston, Virginia, office of the National Principals' Association.

The Association of Secondary School Principals should be commended for its part in fostering these two organizations over the years—the student councils group since the early forties and the Honor Society since 1921. However, today it is incongruous for a principals' association to formulate and control the policies of a national association of student councils.

Evidence of the disenchantment of youth with the National Student Council Association is demonstrated by the diminishing number of schools which affiliate. The 1967 Student Council Handbook claimed membership in "almost 10,000 schools." By 1973, this membership had fallen below 5,000 schools.

The National Honor Society is not working well, either. Local chapters in many high schools have become cliques, producing as much unhappiness as satisfaction. Moreover, the sexual imbalance is severe. In the schools the Commission examined, the membership of the Honor Society was about 80 percent female and 20 percent male. While no official figures are available from the secondary school principals' association, a spokesman advised that girls made up 68 percent of the membership in a limited sample of schools. The Commission does not believe that such results would occur if the students ran the society themselves. Independent funding, new responsibilities, summer programs staffed by students, and activities geared to meet students' needs could make these associations active, independent factors in the high school environment.

NOTES

1. Letter from Thomas Jefferson to Joseph Coolidge, Oct. 13, 1825, Collection of Jefferson Letters, Massachusetts Historical Society, 7th series, vol. 1 (1900).

2. *The School and the Democratic Environment,* a series of papers commissioned by the Danforth Foundation and the Ford Foundation (Columbia University Press: New York, 1970), p. 44.

3. *Tinker v. Des Moines Independent Community School District,* 393 U.S. 503, 506, 511 (1969).

4. *Eisner v. The Stamford Board of Education,* 314 F. Supp. 832 (1970).

5. "Editorial Policy," *Horizon,* a publication of the Lynbrook High School, Lynbrook, N.Y., 1972. Vol. 3, no. 2, Second Issue Dec. 3, 1971.

6. *Hannah v. Larche*, 363 U.S. 420, 442 (1960).

7. *Barker v. Hardway*, 282 F. Supp. 228, 237 (S.D. W. Va. 1968), cert. denied, 394 U.S. 905 (1969).

8. *Givens v. Poe*, D.C.W.D. North Carolina, Charlotte Div., #2615 (June 19, 1972).

9. *Wisconsin v. Yoder*, 406 U.S. 205, 225, 226, 228 (1972).

10. Jerald G. Bachman, Swayzer Green, and Ilona D. Wirtanen, *Dropping Out—Problem or Symptom?* (Ann Arbor, Mich.: Institute for Social Research, 1971), p. 178.

11. *Tinker v. Des Moines Independent Community School District*, italics supplied.

12. Camden, New Jersey, City Ordinance MC 720, adopted Jan. 25, 1973.

13. *Cooper v. Mojunkin*, 4 Ind. 290, 291, 293 (1853).

14. *Ware v. Estes*, 328 F. Supp. 657, 658 (N.D. Tex. 1971), aff'd. 458 F. 2d 1360 (5th Cir. 1972), cert. denied 409 U.S. 1027 (1972).

15. *Guidelines for the Collection, Maintenance, and Dissemination of Pupil Records*, Russell Sage Foundation, Hartford, Conn., March 1970.

CHAPTER 12

Revolt against Sex Stereotypes

Recommendation No. 31: Sexism

School administrators and school boards, at both the state and local levels, must set forth commitments to eliminate all vestiges of sexism in the schools.

Areas of immediate concern are equal employment and treatment of the sexes in instructional and administrative positions, equal opportunities for female students to participate in all curricula areas, including career education, and the elimination of all courses required of only one sex.

Individual teachers should make sure they are not focusing their teaching toward either sex.

All female students who become pregnant should be permitted to remain in school for the full term of pregnancy if they wish to do so and their physician considers it feasible. They should be permitted to return to school following childbirth as soon as released by their physician. There must be no denial of the right to participate in activities because of pregnancy or motherhood, whether the girl is wed or unwed.

Recommendation No. 32: Females in Competitive Team Sports

School boards and administrators at the local level must provide opportunities for female students to participate in programs of competitive team sports that are comparable to the opportunities for males. The programs must be adequately funded through regular school budgets.

Outstanding female athletes must not be excluded from competition as members of male teams in noncontact sports. The fact that a school offers the same team sport for girls should not foreclose this option.

State activities associations should be required by statute to eliminate from their constitutions and bylaws all constraints to full participation in competitive team sports by females.

If state activities associations are to continue to have jurisdiction over female sports, they should be required by state statute to have equal sex representation on all boards supervising boys' and girls' athletics.

Although custom, law, and religion in colonial America tended to consider women as inferior and, therefore, subordinate to men, conditions on the westward-moving frontier had always worked to produce their own kind of equalitarianism. Not only were the traditional women's jobs essential; women were perforce performing men's work. Both the American and the French Revolutions unleashed ideas of equality and natural rights that could not be permanently limited to men. By 1800, behind the frontier, textile production in factories would require women workers as well as men. As a new society took shape in the new world under new and changing conditions, traditional attitudes toward the lot, life, and work of women had to be revised.

Wider educational opportunities for women soon became a focal point for concern. In an essay published in 1790, Mrs. Judith Murray, the daughter of a Gloucester sea captain, asked whether the greater opportunities of young men as against young women were natural circumstances or were produced by "the difference of education and continued advantages."[1] The young Philadelphia physician, Dr. Benjamin Rush, wrote that to keep secure the benefits of the Revolution, ladies "should be qualified to a certain degree by a peculiar education, to concur in instructing their sons in the principles of liberty and government."[2]

Under the stimulus of such concern, the initial sporadic interest in elementary education for girls became a continuing interest in female academies and seminaries, which by the Civil War were to be found in almost every state of the Union. Public high schools or secondary schools where girls might receive an education without paying the fees of the private academies had started up during the first half of the century. By 1890 there were 116,000 girls in public high schools as compared with only 85,000 boys. This was sex-related vocational training: schoolmarms needed high school training, while the most common men's jobs did not.

The second half of the nineteenth century saw a dramatic rise in opportunities for higher education for women and also in the number of women taking advantage of them. Nonsectarian, separate colleges for women were founded in such numbers that in 1880 they were educating almost 30 percent of the women in college. Today, by contrast, single-sex women's colleges enroll approximately 3 percent of the women in higher education.

Unfortunately, educational opportunities for women grew much faster than the number of jobs open to them. In the 1870 census seven occupations accounted for 93 percent of all women workers, and teaching was the only one which called for any considerable education. Women's colleges stressed the general value of the liberal arts for the personal development and social usefulness of their graduates, and did not emphasize either vocational or professional careers, except for teaching.

Economically, they were nearly all marginal operations. Those who were struggling to give women equal educational opportunities often developed a single-mindedness which feared any distractions of energy or interest from their cause. As late as 1900 a suffragette speaker was refused permission to hold a meeting on the campus of a women's college!

On the other hand, emphasis on educational matters came late to the women's movement, which considered discrimination in the schools a much less serious problem than the vote, Prohibition, laws to protect female workers, reform of legislation that restricted married women's rights in family property, and so on. Compared to the rest of society, the schools looked good. There were plenty of women with jobs in schools, even management jobs: in 1928 fifty-five percent of the nation's elementary schools had women principals. By the schools' own measurements, girls did well in school—better than boys.

Not until the 1970s did educators begin to consider the charge that girls are discriminated against throughout their entire educational lives, from kindergarten through graduate school. Among the professional publications which took note of this thesis in the fall of 1972 were the *Reading Teacher*, *The National Elementary Principal*, *The Instructor*, and *Guidepost*, a publication of the American Personnel and Guidance Association. Frequent references were made to the new terms "sexism" and "sexist," words coined around the words "racism" and "racist," referring to discrimination by sex rather than race.

The National Education Association, which had been a traditional advocate of women's rights going back all the way to the time of the suffrage amendment, did not awaken to the seriousness of discrimination in the schools until November of 1972. At that time, the Center for Human Relations of the NEA held a seminar on the problem. Since that time, the

NEA has established a Resource Center of Sex Roles in Education.

The attack on sex discrimination in the schools has emphasized the content of education, and the degree to which school programs acculturate children and adolescents to a society where sex discrimination is pervasive. It has also become increasingly clear that the status of women inside the schools is much less satisfactory than the women's movements of previous generations had thought.

Catherine East, executive secretary of the Citizens' Advisory Council on the Status of Women, pointed out to the Commission that the proportion of elementary schools with women principals had dropped from 55 percent in 1928 to 22 percent in 1968. In the high schools the situation is much worse: only 3 percent of the principals and 9 percent of the assistant principals in American high schools are women. At the top leadership level, women practically disappear: only one-half of 1 percent of the nation's school superintendents are women.

With the spectacular rise in teacher salaries (which jumped 228 percent from 1956 to 1972), men have been competing more aggressively for teaching jobs—and have been winning out over women. There are already more men than women teaching in American high schools, and the trend is still up, supported by the misguided notion that in times of trouble men are better disciplinarians than women. With the large surplus of applicants for teaching jobs that must be anticipated in the next decade, sex discrimination of a kind that is no more than normal in this society will produce a dangerous imbalance.

Even the belief that girls do better than boys in school has come into question. The Educational Testing Service does not make breakdowns by sex of the results on its Scholastic Achievement Tests, but the American College Testing Program supplied the following data for comparative test scores and comparative high school grades:

ACT MEAN SCORES	MEN	WOMEN
English	17.7	19.7
Mathematics	21.0	19.0
Social Studies	20.4	19.2
Natural Sciences	21.6	20.2
Composite	20.3	19.7

HIGH SCHOOL GRADES	MEN	WOMEN
English	2.56	3.04
Mathematics	2.34	2.51
Social Studies	2.76	2.98
Natural Sciences	2.51	2.72
High School Average	2.53	2.80

All the differences are significant.

In a communication to the Commission, Arthur E. Smith, vice president of the Educational Services Division of the American College Testing Program, pointed out that "in every case except English, males did better on the ACT Assessment Battery, yet females reported higher grades. This is subject to several interpretations, one of which might be that high school grading is biased in favor of females or that testing is biased in favor of males. Another possibility is that females may tend to do more of those things that influence grading practices favorably."[3]

The ACT data on the relative superiority of male scores on achievement tests are not borne out by the National Assessment of Educational Progress. J. Stanley Ahmann, staff director of the project, told the Commission that Assessment figures showed female students better than males in reading, writing, literature, and social studies, with males better than females only in science. Moreover, women in college, like girls in high school, get consistently higher grades than males.

One possible explanation of the ACT data is that girls are discriminated against in school as a result of the general assumption that they are doing better work than boys. In coeducational classes, teachers teach to the boys and not to the girls. The justification is that boys are less motivated and require more attention. This teaching strategy is not only discriminatory, but also encourages aggressive male behavior. This approach to teaching was described to the Commission by a superintendent of schools who wrote:

> I have always believed that a teacher of coed classes teaches the males almost to the exclusion of the females present because of the psychology of the situation—the additional motivation necessary to make high school boys want to learn, the high interest level required to sustain them through the class, and the appeal of certain subject matter that is unique to the male. It is always hoped that the girl will be self-stimulated to follow along. This has always been highly discriminatory and is a difficult matter to resolve.[4]

The Commission's national panels of secondary school superintendents, principals, and teachers were polled on this problem and reported as follows:

ADMINISTRATORS' RESPONSE
· 91 percent of the respondents agreed that teachers in their schools or districts direct teaching toward males rather than females in coeducational classes. Reasons cited were reluctance on the part of males to appear interested in the presence of peers and females; males less academically inclined and motivated; the content of subject matter.
· 85 percent of the respondents agreed that teachers in their schools and districts direct more questions to males than to females. Reasons cited were the need to draw reluctant males into discussions; the content of subject matter; the sex of the teacher.

TEACHERS' RESPONSE
· 57 percent of the respondents agreed that they direct their teaching toward males rather than females in coeduca-

tional classes. The reasons cited were the same as those given by the administrators.

· 58 percent of the respondents agreed that they direct more questions to males than to females. Again, the reasons cited were the same as the administrators'.

If girls are not taught in class, and then get higher grades anyway, they will be conditioned to believe that what the school has to teach is not important to them.

Counseling and Vocational Education

According to the Citizens' Advisory Council on the Status of Women, the attitudes of high school counselors act as a brake on the growth of programs and curricula for girls:

> Teacher and counselor attitudes and practices often discourage girls' aspirations and limit their sense of autonomy and self-image. . . . Many counselors and teachers lack information and sensitivity to changing life patterns of women and to widening vocational and higher educational opportunities resulting from changing attitudes and equal opportunity legislation.[5]

Certainly, counselors must accept some of the responsibility for the failure of girls to enroll in science and mathematics courses in the high schools. They must also share the responsibility for the paucity of girls in vocational programs.

BIAS IN VOCATIONAL EDUCATION

Women and girls have been consistently channeled into lower-paying jobs in part because of the expectations of the community, but also in part because of the preparation they have received in high school. As Congresswoman Patsy Mink said in introducing her bill entitled the Women's Education Act of 1972 into the House:

> Our educational system has divided the sexes into an insidious form of role-playing. Women provide the services and men exploit them. Women are the secretaries, nurses,

teachers, and domestics, and men are the bosses, doctors, professors, and foremen. Textbooks, media, curriculum, testing, counseling, and so forth, are all based on the correctness of this division of labor, and serve to reinforce the sex-role stereotype that is so devastating for our postindustrial society. More importantly, this division of labor according to sex is a totally false assumption of roles.[6]

Girls and women desperately need opportunities to improve their employment positions and to move into new careers. The secondary school should become a significant force for increasing the earning ability and status of women and girls.

Statistics on the number of girls in vocational high school programs, however, continue to be disheartening. According to the U.S. Department of Labor:

> More than half of the women and girls in public vocational programs are being trained in home economics; about one-third are studying office practices. Very few are being prepared for trades and industry, health occupations, or technical jobs.[7]

Yet opportunities in all these areas are opening for women.

Today, the practice of channeling girls into limited occupational areas is not merely disgraceful; it is illegal. The Comprehensive Help Manpower Training Act of 1971 includes the following provision:

> The Secretary [of Health, Education, and Welfare] may not enter into a contract under this title with any school unless the school furnishes assurances satisfactory to the Secretary that it will not discriminate on the basis of sex in the admission of individuals to its training programs.[8]

Since practically all vocational programs are at least partially supported by federal funding, there must be an enormous amount of noncompliance about which nothing is being done.

A contributing factor to the lack of vocational programs for girls is a graduation requirement of vocational homemaking education for girls, still enforced by many states. This requirement can be met only by the sacrifice of instructional time which could be more profitably used for other purposes. While some progress is being made, and a number of schools have recently dropped the vocational home economics requirement, many school systems continue this discriminatory rule. Too many old-fashioned vocational educators still conceive of the woman's working role as primarily domestic, and feel that time spent on technical training for girls is wasted because girls marry and leave their jobs. However, the average woman worker stays employed for twenty-five years, as against forty-three years for the average male worker; and the single woman averages forty-five years in the labor force.

Vocational educators should realize that the entire technical area must be open to high school girls. There is no question that they can do the work, if asked.

> Women have studied engineering in American colleges almost as long as men. Ellen Swallow took engineering-related courses at M.I.T. in 1871. Edith Griswold enrolled in engineering at New York City's Normal College in 1886. Yet women comprised then, and still comprise today, less than one percent of annual engineering graduates.

> Women in engineering in this country represent something of a paradox. Employers rate women engineers high in performance. Women engineers rate engineering high as a profession. Yet women comprise less than one percent of academically trained engineers.[9]

It is this sort of discrimination the schools must work to stop.

Sexism

Action to correct disparities in the schooling of boys and girls must be taken at all levels of the educational enterprise. Reform can be accomplished only by the joint efforts of the legislature, state departments of education, school boards, and local high schools. Perhaps the most extensive prescription of the work to be done has been set out in a memorandum to administrators by John C. Pittenger, secretary of education for the Commonwealth of Pennsylvania. His requirements were as follows:

1. Sex-segregated and sex-stereotyped classes, programs, activities, and courses of study be eliminated.

2. Feminist literature be included in school libraries and efforts be made to secure instructional materials, including textbooks, which favorably portray women in nontraditional roles.

3. All students be counseled to consider a variety of career opportunities, not only those traditionally entered by persons of their sex.

4. Job placement practices assure students of employment opportunities without restriction because of sex.

5. Annual goals be set for hiring, training, and promoting women of all races at every level of employment.

6. The role of women becomes an integral part of the school curriculum.

I recommend you develop programs, if you have not already done so, such as the following to support these policies.

1. Sensitize all staff to sexism and to what are degrading and discriminatory practices.

2. Eliminate sex-stereotyped roles in all school publications.

3. Eliminate assignments by sex in all job classes and student positions.

4. Seek the establishment of child care/development programs for children of staff, faculty, and students, with costs according to ability to pay. These programs can be used for training the students in child care and family relationships.

5. Provide before and after school programs especially for children whose parents work.

6. Provide a sex education course in human growth and development which includes emotional and physical growth and interpersonal relationships.[10]

The Issue of Pregnancy

Studies conducted by the staff of the Commission confirm that most high schools still enforce discriminatory regulations against female students who become pregnant. The general attitude of secondary educators is that pregnant girls should not be seen in school. Most schools either require them to drop out or refer them to a center for pregnant girls. School systems without special centers usually suggest that schooling be continued in adult education evening programs.

There are no centers for pregnant girls that offer a program comparable to that of a regular high school. The staff of the Commission could not find a single center which offered chemistry, physics, or advanced mathematics.

When schools force pregnant girls to leave high school, they are operating outside the law. Court decisions have consistently held that pregnant students, married or unmarried, can neither be excluded from high school nor relegated to special or adult programs.

High school girls who become pregnant must have the opportunity to continue in the regular high school if they wish to do so. An individual student may prefer to attend a special program; that should be her decision. The choice must be that of the student, and the school should not become involved, even in a counseling capacity.

Girls' Athletics

One of the most obvious areas of discrimination against girls is secondary school athletics, where opportunities in both individual and team sports are either second-rate or nonexistent.

The Commission takes the position that girls should receive the same encouragement, opportunities, and aspirations as boys to become involved in the excitement of team and individual sports. Furthermore, girls' programs should have equal use of all physical facilities. There are too many cases where girls are not allowed to use a gymnasium during basketball season, or the girls' gym is invariably selected for social events while the boys' gym is carefully guarded for boys' basketball or male sports.

Under the present system of operation, most high schools completely segregate boys' and girls' physical education except in the teaching of modern dance. The Commission believes that both sexes will benefit if physical education classes are coeducational. Schools should offer opportunities for the sexes to compete in noncontact sports, especially in sports with adult carry-over value such as tennis, swimming, golf, archery, and so on.

An extreme example of sex discrimination in the schools is the pay differential between women who coach girls' sports and men who coach comparable sports for boys. Women coaches of girls' sports receive between one-third and one-half the salary of men who coach boys. This disparity results from the biased manner in which school boards classify various sports for salary supplements. All sports activities for girls are classified as minor, while most activities for boys are classified as major. School boards must act to end this discrimination.

STATE HIGH SCHOOL ACTIVITIES ASSOCIATIONS

High school athletics are administered by state high school associations. These associations are controlled largely by high school principles and coaches. A review of the handbook of the National Federation of State High School Athletic Associations indicates that they have historically acted to restrain participation by high school girls in athletic contests. For example, the 1970–71 handbook said about girls' athletics:

> That a competition should be confined to reasonably limited areas and that provisions should be made for friendly, social activities in connection with any competitive event.[11]

The next year, suddenly, the Federation saw the light, and the 1972 handbook offered the following pronouncement:

Interscholastic athletics for girls are being sponsored by an increasing number of secondary schools and consequently by state high school associations. There is a trend toward expansion of girls interscholastic competitive opportunities in athletics in virtually all states. This is due to the belief that schools need to provide girls with challenging outlets for physical activity when their needs require more than intramural programs. For three decades, educators avoided sponsoring interscholastic programs for girls because of cultural restrictions and physiological half-truths. Many parents believed it was unladylike to participate in athletics and that girls who did became large, muscular, and non-feminine in appearance. *This assumption has no validity.* From the viewpoint of equality of opportunity, girls are just as entitled to competitive experiences as are boys. If athletics are beneficial, they must be good for girls as well as boys. Recently, the American Medical Association released the results of a study pointing out that the health benefits of wholesome exercise are as great for women as they are for men. It announced that women who maintain a high level of health and fitness can meet family and career responsibilities more effectively and can pursue avocational interests more enjoyably.[12]

In fact, the Federation began to move only after the courts proceeded to strike down the rules barring females from participation in interscholastic athletics. Unfortunately, it still advocates totally separate programs for girls, even though district courts in several cases have ruled that girls must be allowed to participate as members of boys' teams in noncontact sports.

In April 1973, the United States Court of Appeals ruled that the Minnesota State High School League had violated the equal protection clause of the Fourteenth Amendment by barring females from participating with males in noncontact interscholastic athletics. The schools involved were ordered to let girls try out for the teams, and the State High School League was enjoined from imposing any sanctions upon the schools involved, or upon any schools competing against them.[13]

On the basis of this decision, the Commission is confident that the National Federation will revise its constitution and bylaws to grant equal rights of participation in interscholastic athletics to females.

Nevertheless, the Commission has strong reservations about the ability of this group to administer interscholastic athletics for girls. Nationwide, the group is practically all male and has little or no female participation on its national or state boards. Either the Activities Associations should be restructured to provide comparable representation for both sexes on their boards of directors, or some other agency, such as the state department of education, should take over the function of supervising athletics for female students.

If equality of the sexes is to be accomplished in the high schools, local school boards must increase the funding of programs for girls or reallocate funds which presently favor programs for boys. This is especially true in the areas of vocational education and sports. The changes in policy which are necessary to eliminate sex bias from the schools require insistence and a strong stand. In this area, as in so many of the others this Commission has explored, the most effective pressure will come from the involvement of citizens at the local level.

NOTES

1. Eleanor Flexner, *Century of Struggle* (Cambridge, Mass.: Harvard University Press, 1959), p. 16, n. 21.

2. Ibid., p. 17, n. 24.

3. Letter to the Commission from Arthur E. Smith, vice president, Educational Services Division, the American College Testing Program, Oct. 23, 1972.

4. Sister Caroleen Hensgen, superintendent of schools, Diocese of Dallas, in response to Inquiry No. 2 of the National Panel of Secondary Principals and Superintendents.

5. Citizens' Advisory Council on the Status of Women, *Need for Studies of Sex Discrimination in Public Schools* (Washington, D.C.: Government Printing Office, 1972), pp. 1, 5.

6. *Congressional Record*, 92d Cong., 2d Sess., Apr. 18, 1972, p. H-3259.

7. Women's Bureau, Employment Standards Administration, U.S. Department of Labor, *Help Improve Vocational Education for Women and Girls in Your Community* (Washington, D.C.: Government Printing Office, 1971), p. 1.

8. Section 110 of Public Law 92-157 and Section 11 of Public Law 92-158.

9. John B. Parrish, "Are There Women in Engineering's Future?" *AAUW Journal*, vol. 59, no. 1, pp. 29, 31, October 1965.

10. "Sexism in Education," School Administrators' Memorandum 544, Commonwealth of Pennsylvania Department of Education, Sept. 5, 1972.

11. National Federation of State High School Athletic Associations Official Handbook 1970–71, p. 62, 1970.

12. "Recommendations," National Federation of State High School Athletic Associations Official Handbook, 1972–73, p. 28, 1972.

13. *Brenden v. Independent School District 742*, No. 72-1287 (8th Cir., Apr. 18, 1973).

PART VI

ISSUES
AND
DISSENT

CHAPTER 13

Issues Yet To Be Resolved

Much of what was discussed in the meetings of the National
Commission on the Reform of Secondary Education has not
found a place in the pages of this report. The Commissioners
were deeply concerned about the financial future of the nation's schools, and about the means that could be found to pay
the bills. The educational and societal problems that fall under
the words "integration," "racial balance," and "bussing," were
omnipresent at the table. One half-day session was devoted
to presentations on "performance-based teacher education,"
and one of the few subjects on which there was immediate
and continuing agreement was the need for root-and-branch
reform in teacher education.

These were not, in the end, the subjects with which the
Commission had to deal by the nature of its mandate. Other
commissions have recently reported on or are currently ex-
ploring the financial picture. Integration is front-and-center
before the courts, the legislatures, and the public. Only a few
extremists in any of the races would now deny the desirability
of the goal, but only a few enthusiasts believe that the way
to the goal is known. While the Commission did not treat

these debates as separate entities in its report, discussions relating to them are dispersed throughout the report. Several of the recommendations, hopefully, will contribute toward the resolution of these issues.

Money, race, and teacher preparation are all subjects closer to newspaper coverage of education than many of the subjects dealt with in this report, but that does not make them more fundamental. If the recommendations for reform contained in this report are carried through, the Commission believes that most other matters will fall in place—or at least they will become manageable. A community more deeply involved in the educational process might be more willing to spend what it costs; a system of alternative schools with voluntary attendance above the age of fourteen could provide a new focus for integration; and both these developments would make teachers more cognizant of the adequacy of their preparation.

What counts are the goals and objectives, and the results. The Commission is confident of its goals and objectives, and looks forward to seeing results.

CHAPTER 14

Memoranda of Reservation or Dissent

Complete agreement among twenty individuals on the controversial issue of how best to change secondary education is neither likely nor desirable. At its first meeting, the Commission agreed that it would reach consensus where possible but where there were notable points of difference or even strong disagreements, the issue would not be avoided but rather provision made for individual dissent.

The memoranda of comment, reservation, and dissent by individual commission members adds flavor to the report and gives further insight into some of the more disputatious issues dealt with by the Commission.

We urge that this section be read carefully.

B. FRANK BROWN
Chairman

Page 3, paragraph 3—By John A. Stanavage
Perhaps the most indefensible statement in the report is the reference to a "rapidly changing society and a slowly

167

changing school." What is missing in both our society and our schools at this point is a definite sense of direction. Sporadic changes, perhaps better called mutations, are occurring in society as in our schools, but up to the present these changes have summated mainly in greater confusion and chaos.

Our schools are in disarray because our society also is wracked by uncertainty. Once our nation regains some common sense of mission and purpose, its schools will help it realize its goals, as they have done so well in the past.

Page 5, paragraph 3—By John A. Stanavage

I think the threat to the comprehensive high school is much overdrawn. (The percentage figure, of course, is completely chimerical.) Not that a drop in enrollment in the standard high school may not occur as other educational alternatives become available to young people, but that quite misses the point. No educator is seeking to perpetuate any particular form of schooling. The important thing is that there will be masses of young people seeking education tomorrow and in the 1970s and in the 1980s. If the comprehensive high school can meet their demands, fine. If not, American education has the ingenuity and the resilience to develop other formats of schooling that will do so.

Page 12—By Martin Mayer

I do not think the source of failure in Title I programs has been the lack of "diagnosis or concern for individual problems." If we could manage the group problems, the individual problems would mostly disappear.

Page 16, Recommendation No. 12—By Martin Mayer

Adolescents cannot do this, and asking them to attempt it is no kindness to them.

Page 18, Recommendation No. 20—By Thomas C. Mendenhall

More in sorrow than in anger, and out of a concern that the dilemma of any college or university which must somehow select among its applicants should at least be mentioned, I must comment on, if not dissent from, this recommendation.

The limitations and liabilities of rank in class must be agreed to by all, based as it is on "arbitrary and competitive grades." But even the Commission must recognize that rank in class has in fact proved a most useful predictor in many cases. And to do away with it at this particular time, especially with the pious recognition that "other predictors . . . might be more subtle and more difficult to compute" is almost irresponsible!

Traditionally, three measurements or predictors have been used in varying combinations for college admission: school grades and rank in class, national tests, and personal recommendations from teachers and administrators. In recent years the courts have rendered the last much less revealing and useful. National tests are under increasing criticism on several counts from many quarters. And now grades are being blurred with the popularity of Pass-Fail and with grade-point averages to be dropped, if the Commission is listened to.

If the above analysis is at all true, it is imperative that all involved (schools and colleges, students and teachers, testers and administrators) work together to simplify the process and stem the torrent of paper flooding in from each student which seems the only alternative at present.

Page 21, Recommendation No. 28—By Rosalie C. Risinger

Until there is more evidence that schools, community, and/ or business will develop and provide "other programs to accommodate those who wish to leave school," I cannot support this recommendation to drop school leaving age to fourteen.

We must provide the leadership in developing programs

and assume more accountability in meeting the educational needs of all people.

Page 21, Recommendation No. 31—By Martin Mayer
I dissent from the use of the foolish word "sexism."

Page 33—By John A. Stanavage
While I would not quarrel with the goal of "appreciation for others," I do not think that it stresses sufficiently the imperative obligation of the school to help young people prepare for satisfactory life in a richly pluralistic society. I am also concerned that reference is made to ethnic and religious diversity, but not to racial, cultural, and socioeconomic differences. This seems an odd, a crucial omission at this stage in our national life.

Page 33, Knowledge of Self Goal—By Martin Mayer
I cannot accept the conventional wisdom that a "positive self-image" is always desirable. Usually it is a lie. Moreover, it is probably incompatible with religious belief. Those who ask "What is man that Thou are mindful of him?" are more likely to be wise and to manage their behavior decently than those who achieve a "positive self-image." A degree of humility is not incompatible with a belief that one can get things done, or with doing them.

Page 42, paragraph 4, and page 63—By Thomas C. Mendenhall
"Drastic content revision in the social studies" and "the new course in global studies." Again, I would only remind my friends on the Commission who do not happen to be historians or social scientists of the magnitude of our hopes here and the difficulties that surround their achievements.

In the last decade much has been done to introduce materials from such social sciences as economics and anthropology into secondary school courses. But the difficulties encountered so far should make us more realistic in our efforts to create global studies. Not only must university scholars be enlisted to prepare new materials, teacher-training programs be reordered, school curricula revised (and not simply augmented!), and classroom teachers assisted to acquire new information and new approaches, but also these vital steps must be done concurrently and cooperatively if the effort is to be successful.

Page 44, paragraph 4—By John A. Stanavage

The limitations of performance-based instruction in all learning situations are insufficiently stated in this section of the report. The quest for measurable objectives has resulted in too many cases in the trivialization of learning. While no one could object to the formulation of clear objectives for the learning tasks placed before young people, the nature, the quality, and the worth of those objectives are of paramount importance. Moreover, education is more than conditioning or programming, at least as we aspire for it in our democratic society.

The evidence is insufficient as yet as to whether performance-based instruction is really the wave of the future, or simply another specious contribution by the great simplifiers. Under any circumstances, we must make certain we do not forfeit our fundamental goals in our efforts to devise easily obtainable objectives.

Page 46—By Martin Mayer

I dissent from the paragraph about history texts, though I recognize that what it says is almost universally accepted. The most dangerous fallacies are the most popular. In fact, the great bulk of the history of the United States before the late nineteenth century was made by male white Protestants. It

may be regarded as unwise to write history textbooks truth-
fully (and they are not now truthful, anyway), but if we are
demanding propaganda rather than history we should have
the guts to say so.

Page 53—By Thomas C. Mendenhall

The Post-High School Dropout Problem. Again, I would
only regret that the Commission did not have time to push
its analysis of the problem far enough. The figures on post-
high school dropouts are indeed serious for the students, for
the colleges, and for society as a whole. Better training in
job-entry skills and better career components in secondary
schools (which the Commission supports) are an important,
promising answer.

But the fact is that many of these students have dropped
out because college, *as presently defined,* in such a limited
fashion, is not the place for them. Yet some kind of post-
secondary experience may well be needed in their case. To
create such variations and to make society at large appreciate
and support a wide range of post-secondary alternatives, including colleges, is surely the more complete answer.

Page 53, The College Dropout—By Martin Mayer

I do not consider the college dropout a problem case, and
I am unable to understand why either former Congressman
Pucinski or my colleagues do. College dropouts are quickly
employed, and are usually happier at work than they were at
college. They are much less likely than high school dropouts
to be placed in dead-end situations. In most cases, the new
college graduate is no better equipped for job-hunting than
the dropout.

Page 58, "Fulfilling Occupation"—By Martin Mayer

The emphasis on "careers" that are "fulfilling" seems to me
a weasel. In ancient Athens, the plantation South, and modern

Switzerland, educators could assume that slaves or foreigners would do the dirty work, and could build up expectations in others for fulfillment on the job. This country, one hopes, does not want slaves. As the do-it-yourself householder knows, any job well done gives pleasure in the doing; but most people still in one way or another earn their bread by the sweat of their brow, and the fulfillment given by the job is the wages. We need garbage men; the garbage man who is confident of the importance of his work and performs it efficiently is probably a happier garbage man; but the "work itself," to use the Bell System slogan, is not likely to be "fulfilling." This is an argument for making it pay well.

Page 69, Foreign Languages—By Martin Mayer

I think the Commission has been much too complacent about the tragedy of foreign language teaching. The universal acceptance of English as a *lingua franca* will not, I think, last through the working lives of the adolescents of the next decade. Worse, I think it entirely impossible to break out of the prison of ethnocentricity without knowing enough of at least one foreign language to understand that the thought processes necessary to work in that language are rather different from those you use in your own. Foreign language learning correlates least of all subjects with the social class status of students (we actually promote bilingual education among the poorest of the poor in New Mexico and Southern California). It would be the ideal vehicle for academic emphasis among the unlucky.

Moreover, I do not find anything positive in the need for language teachers to scramble for students. The beginning phases of language instruction are drudgery: the time horizon of most adolescents is not long enough to allow victory to the teacher who must offer drudgery today for the sake of an educated life tomorrow. I would urge restoration of a language requirement for entry into four-year colleges as a necessary first step in the restoration of language teaching to its proper importance in the secondary school.

Page 85, "Action-Learning"—By Martin Mayer

I object to the use of the sales-pitch term "action-learning." It has no meaning not already covered by "voluntary experience." Its function in the educational community is to give an air of novelty to an old (and very simple) idea. To the outside world, the term "action-learning" is yet another example of that baby-jargon that has made the study of education a target for ridicule and contempt in the intellectual community. Finally, the statement that learning is "immediately reinforced" in the unstructured and ambiguous situation of the social service agency strikes me as astonishingly untrue.

Chapter 9, pages 97–111—By John A. Stanavage

In the editing of this chapter, a substantive change in emphasis has occurred. The Commission's advocacy of a wide spectrum of educational alternatives for young people was not based originally on the sophomoric assumption that the conventional high school has failed. Rather it was founded on the realization that no single model of American secondary school could suffice any longer to meet all the variegated needs of America's pluralistic society and its highly diversified youth.

Pages 99–109—"Alternativeness"—By Martin Mayer

I object bitterly to this recommendation. Let "secondary educators" consider student interests and capabilities, the requirements of diverse jobs and careers, the strength and beauty of academic disciplines, even the organization of school bureaucracies—but, please God, not "alternativeness," which if it means anything at all means merely difference for its own sake.

What distresses me is my feeling that an important idea is being destroyed in this chapter and out in the real world of schools, too. I have always believed in the provision of different kinds of schools, based essentially on the interest of the people (teachers as well as students) who must do the work. There should be conservatories staffed by musicians and artists for the musically and artistically inclined. There should be science schools that stress health services, others that stress mathematics, others that stress technology. I want to see commercial high schools, industrial high schools, high schools that train specifically for entry into the larger civil services, or telecommunications, or the military. Academic studies need not be slighted at such schools. At my urging, the Commission visited a school in New York City for which students are selected *solely* on artistic ability, represent the full racial and nearly the full income and intellectual range of the city, take three hours a day in studio work in some area of commercial art or design—and in overwhelming proportion (80 percent) move on to some form of higher education. That is for me an entirely valid alternative to the comprehensive high school: it has purposes understood by all involved.

But "alternativeness" is all airy-fairy. Significantly, it says nothing to *teaching*: indeed, the thrust of this chapter and of Chapter 7 is against *teaching*: students are to teach themselves, while teachers "diagnose." What we are dealing with here, in fact, is the administrator's and bureaucrat's view of education. The Vicar of Bray is amongst us.

One of my colleagues on the Commission expressed astonishment at my reaction to this chapter, because I had agreed that there are different "cognitive styles" in learning. So there are —different mediating structures are efficient in differing degrees for different students. Some learn best from verbal mediation, some from pictures, some from hands on concrete objects; and all styles are valid. Fitting the presentation to the student is the teacher's job. Moving the teacher and student to some purposeless "alternative school" will not make that job any easier, and may indeed obscure it behind a rush of irrelevant stimuli. School is not and should not be a T-group.

I have, God wot, no great faith in classrooms. I have not been in one for the purpose of learning what the teacher was supposed to teach since I was eighteen years old, and during the three preceding years at Harvard I attended considerably less than one-quarter of all the classes I was supposed to attend. Harvard did not think this is a good idea, and Harvard was right: a lot of it was just being a twerp. But they finally left me alone, because in my twerp way I was acquiring my own education, and there was at least a chance that it would be viable for me.

One of the worst things about American education has been its simple-minded faith that you can find out what an educated man knows and does ("critical thinking," etc.) and then teach *that*. You can't. Assuming that there is something to this chapter beyond an attempt to resurrect the discredited Yahoo progressivism of the 1950s (which is a charitable assumption), it seems to call for a structuring of education that makes students do what people who educate themselves have always done. Real diversity of purpose, ability, background, and taste have been left out entirely, though they are the stimulators of self-education and the reason for diversity of schooling. What is being proposed here won't work; and the less resourceful the student, the greater the harm that will be done.

Page 106, Aid Formulas—By Martin Mayer

It seems to me that the substitution of "register" for "attendance" in the aid formula is profound social folly. The schools push out too many kids already, and one of the few restraining factors is that each dismissal, formal or informal, costs the system money. If the schools can keep the money without the student, there will be a holocaust of "trouble-makers."

Page 109, Rank in Class—By Martin Mayer

I worry about the elimination of grade-point averages and rank in class, because I think that in real life the result will be to make a student's chance of acceptance entirely a function of his standardized test score. Let me note that it also seems at least possible that the junior colleges receiving the product of alternative schools will have to deal with some unusual weaknesses as well as the "unusual strengths."

Pages 115–125, The Crisis in School Security—By John A. Stanavage

The importance of security in our schools and of the current threats to it is not to be minimized. Hence I find myself in the main to be in accord with this chapter. Nevertheless, it must be stressed that many schools, perhaps most schools, are not confronted with the serious problems vividly portrayed here. The Commission would be guilty of irresponsible alarmism if it left the impression that terror is stalking the halls of all our high schools.

The problem is a real and urgent one for certain schools. But the incomprehension of so many working school administrators when presented with the issue gave eloquent testimony that these untoward conditions are not prevalent in all schools.

Page 116—By Martin Mayer

(Bailey statement) It is simply not true that disruption and injustice are correlated. Mussolini's Italy, contemporary Mexico, and the Soviet Union, to take only three, are models of exceedingly unjust societies that show great tranquillity. Even the argument that an unjust society can achieve tranquillity only by paying a high price in repression really does not wash. English society is much less just than American society (the whole working class are still niggers in England), and much more tranquil. Many societies with strong commitments to social justice—Uruguay, the "Sweden of the Americas," is a prime example—have been torn apart by violent disruption. The point is worth making because Bailey's prescrpition frees the school from duties it should be made to fulfill.

Page 119, paragraph 7—By John A. Stanavage

The restrictions against smoking by students are almost impossible to enforce in any school. However, since there is no doubt that smoking is deleterious to health, for the school to give sanction to smoking is to abdicate its educational role. Moreover, as any experienced school man will substantiate, the existence of a student smoking lounge does little to abate smoking in the rest rooms.

Under no circumstances could I endorse this recommendation.

Page 125—By Martin Mayer

I do not believe action-learning programs will help reduce crime. To the extent that adolescents with criminal experience are assigned to such "community-based learning experiences," it would behoove the school to be ready to handle angry questions from the community and severe attacks in the press.

Page 128, Recommendation No. 30: Youth Organizations—By Edwin B. Keim

Recommendation No. 30 may seem to have some basis of logic on first reading. There are, however, facts that must be carefully considered before such a recommendation is implemented.

The National Association of Student Councils and the National Honor Society have long been sponsored by the National Association of Secondary School Principals and have their counterparts in state and local organizations. Each activity is under the direction of the Student Activities Committee of

NASSP. This committee is composed of seven adults (principals or student council sponsors) and seven students, each having equal voting rights. The students have a full voice, and no attempt is made by NASSP to dominate the activities of either organization.

The basic purpose of the NASC is to bring the students and the school administrators into a working relationship which will be to the advantage of the students and the school. The aim of the NHS is to bring recognition to students for outstanding scholarship and also for service, leadership, and evidence of character. Each school has wide discretion in the administration of the school's chapter of the NHS.

It should be further noted that NASSP invests several hundred thousand dollars in the operation of the two organizations annually, and this is done in keeping with the aim of NASSP to be of service to youth. Not only does NASSP invest considerable funds in the operations of the NASC and the NHS, but the two organizations have full use of the editing, publishing, and legal services of NASSP.

Should NASSP withdraw its support from the NASC and NHS, the immediate result would be the demise of both organizations, as each depends upon NASSP for a great part of its funding.

It should also be noted that certain profit-sharing organizations are already in the wings, and if NASSP should lay aside the sponsorship of the NASC and the NHS these organizations would certainly move in and operate the activities for private gain.

It must also be noted that through the sponsorship of the two organizations NASSP makes available some $200,000 annually in scholarships to outstanding students.

Certainly an arrangement that has worked so well for so long with benefits to students should not be laid aside lightly.

The writer does believe that the qualification of character for membership in the NHS should be examined, not because the presence of character is not a worthy condition, but because of the difficulty in measuring the quality.

Page 128, Recommendation No. 30—By John A. Stanavage

While I would agree that neither the student council nor the honor society is a major force in our schools today, I think the connection between their importance and their sponsorship by the NASSP is exiguous at best. The Commission would have been better advised to have studied the role and nature of student involvement in school governance and the place of honor societies in the contemporary American school, rather than settling on such an easy but tangential solution.

Page 129—By Martin Mayer

The Danforth-Ford Study: I do not think all principals—or even most—automatically side with teachers who come complaining about students. In the context of the principal's office, it is the teacher, not the student, who is making trouble at that moment. The principal wants the teacher to handle the problem himself, to go away and stop bothering him about this student, and this attitude often shows.

Pages 133–136, Compulsory Schooling—By John A. Stanavage

Only most reluctantly would I accept this recommendation to lower the compulsory schooling age to fourteen, and then only with certain precautions that are not stated explicitly in this report. That the compulsory aspects of school attendance and other school regulations are incompatible with a meaningful adolescence for many of our young people is not to be denied. Attempting to keep these young people within the confines of the school and apart from adult society has proved to be counterproductive. Thus reducing the school leaving age to fourteen might be therapeutic.

However, unless concern is taken to provide those early school-leavers with alternative forms of education and appropriate counseling once having left school, all we shall be doing is to doom them to economic and educational inferiority. Low-order work in our culture is not stimulating, not educative in itself. Untrained youth fares ill on the job market today. Simply adding to that pool will exacerbate rather than ameliorate the situation.

Certainly our young people should have the option to seek their education either within schools or out in life itself. But our task as educators—and the responsibility of the larger society—is to see that the young person continues to grow in understandings, skills, and knowledge, so that he does not foreclose his own future.

Page 138—By Martin Mayer

In regard to the Camden rule on parental liability: As local school board chairman and as visitor to the juvenile courts, I have seen a number of parents whose necks I would gladly wring, but I fear that what Camden has tried will do more harm than good. Much of what is wrong with these kids is in their relations with their parents. The rule that says that mischief in school will get the old man in trouble may be more an incentive than a barrier to misbehavior.

Page 139—By Martin Mayer

The one month's service students are to donate in return for "free education" beyond the age of fourteen would have a cash value if they did not donate it. It is, in fact, a fee to be paid. Like any fee, it discriminates against poor students, who could use this time to help pay the family bills. I sympathize with the reasoning that led the Commission to this proposal, but I cannot endorse it.

Page 142—By Martin Mayer

Mental health records should not be shown to students or parents without the consent of the physician who caused the entries to be placed in the file.

Page 155—By Martin Mayer

I dissent from all the unkind words about homemaking courses. There is already too much malnutrition caused by ignorance rather than by poverty; we should not seek to increase it. Obviously, these courses should be offered equally to both sexes.

General Dissent—By John A. Stanavage

I object to the tone of the report which intimates that the standard high school has failed completely its educational and social mission. This is a serious misreading of the actual situation. Moreover, it is a mindless return to the tired rhetoric of the past decade when any pied-piper critic could muster a quick audience by hurling gratuitous and unfounded charges against the schools.

The schools of America are far from perfect; they fall short of their own aspirations. But they have served and are serving American society well. It is not any floridly alleged failure of our schools that now makes their own reform imperative, but rather strong evolutionary forces in both our schools and our society that make purposeful change the order of the day.

It is my impression that the Commission was in the main affirmative in its assessment of the American secondary school today and sought to discern those new directions it should pursue. Unfortunately, the report does not reflect that positive attitude.

APPENDIXES

APPENDIX A   COMPARISON OF RESULTS OF NATIONAL GOALS SURVEY

GOALS	PANEL RESPONDING	ESSENTIAL Percent	IMPORTANT BUT NOT ESSENTIAL Percent	OF SECONDARY IMPORTANCE Percent	NOT CHIEFLY THE RESPONSIBILITY OF THE SCHOOL Percent	PANEL'S RATING OF RECENT GRADUATES
Respect for law and authority	Principals and superintendents	77.0	16.5	3.0	3.5	6.4
	Teachers	61.0	25.5	7.9	5.6	6.0
	Parents	75.0	12.2	2.1	10.7	6.1
	Students	49.0	21.6	14.7	14.7	5.7
Clarification of values	Principals and superintendents	70.0	23.0	4.5	2.5	6.0
	Teachers	70.0	25.5	1.7	2.8	5.9
	Parents	62.9	19.3	3.6	14.2	5.9
	Students	41.4	31.2	14.0	13.4	5.2
Adjustment to change	Principals and superintendents	67.3	30.3	1.0	1.4	5.9
	Teachers	59.3	27.1	10.7	2.9	5.7
	Parents	57.1	26.4	7.9	8.6	6.2
	Students	48.4	32.5	8.3	10.8	6.2

Nature and environment					
Principals and superintendents	43.3	44.7	11.5	0.5	5.95
Teachers	47.5	42.9	9.6	0.0	5.8
Parents	42.9	38.6	15.7	2.8	5.7
Students	35.7	40.2	19.1	5.0	6.0
Appreciation of others					
Principals and superintendents	69.0	23.0	4.5	3.5	6.0
Teachers	69.5	25.5	3.9	1.1	6.2
Parents	57.1	26.4	7.9	8.6	6.2
Students	58.6	25.5	6.4	9.5	6.2
Economic understanding					
Principals and superintendents	57.7	32.0	7.8	2.5	5.6
Teachers	38.4	41.3	15.8	4.5	5.4
Parents	48.6	35.7	13.6	2.1	5.5
Students	33.1	35.7	26.1	5.1	5.4
Communication skills					
Principals and superintendents	91.0	8.0	1.0	0.0	6.0
Teachers	90.4	9.0	0.0	0.6	6.6
Parents	92.9	7.1	0.0	0.0	7.4
Students	81.5	16.5	1.3	0.7	6.6

APPENDIX A COMPARISON OF RESULTS OF NATIONAL GOALS SURVEY (Continued)

GOALS	PANEL RESPONDING	ESSENTIAL Percent	IMPORTANT BUT NOT ESSENTIAL Percent	OF SECONDARY IMPORTANCE Percent	NOT CHIEFLY THE RESPONSIBILITY OF THE SCHOOL Percent	PANEL'S RATING OF RECENT GRADUATES
Knowledge of self	Principals and superintendents	89.0	11.0	0.0	0.0	6.5
	Teachers	82.0	14.7	1.1	2.2	6.2
	Parents	70.0	19.3	0.7	10.0	6.2
	Students	65.0	22.3	4.5	8.2	6.2
Responsibility for citizenship	Principals and superintendents	86.6	12.4	1.0	0.0	6.6
	Teachers	76.3	18.7	3.4	1.6	6.3
	Parents	82.0	16.5	0.0	1.5	6.5
	Students	62.4	26.8	7.6	3.2	6.3
Critical thinking	Principals and superintendents	82.6	17.4	0.0	0.0	6.0
	Teachers	83.6	15.3	1.1	0.0	6.0
	Parents	89.3	8.6	0.0	2.1	6.3
	Students	80.3	15.9	2.5	1.3	6.5

Occupational competence	Principals and superintendents	62.0	36.0	1.1	0.9	6.0
	Teachers	48.6	38.4	10.2	2.8	6.0
	Parents	69.3	23.6	5.0	2.1	6.0
	Students	68.1	22.3	7.7	1.9	6.2
Computation skills	Principals and superintendents	53.0	37.2	9.3	0.5	6.7
	Teachers	45.7	40.1	13.7	0.5	6.6
	Parents	68.6	26.4	5.0	0.0	6.6
	Students	47.8	39.4	11.5	1.3	6.7
The achievements of man	Principals and superintendents	43.3	44.7	11.5	0.5	5.95
	Teachers	47.5	42.9	9.6	0.0	5.8
	Parents	42.9	38.6	15.7	2.8	5.7
	Students	35.7	40.2	19.1	5.0	6.0

APPENDIX B   NATIONAL GOALS IN HISTORICAL PERSPECTIVE

CARDINAL PRINCIPLES OF 1918	NATIONAL GOALS OF 1973
Health (Physical Fitness)	Adjustment to Change (Mental Health)
Command of Fundamental Processes	Communication Skills Computation Skills
Vocation	Occupational Competence
Civic Education	Responsibility for Citizenship Respect for Law and Authority Appreciation of Others
Worthy Home Membership Worthy Use of Leisure Ethical Character	Knowledge of Self Critical Thinking Clarification of Values Economic Understanding The Achievements of Man Nature and Environment

----- (Broken Line)—Separates interrelated goals
——— (Solid Line)—Separates unrelated goals